Critical Thinking for Business Students

Second Edition

Linda Dyer

D1402521

Captus Press

Critical Thinking for Business Students, Second Edition

Captus Press Inc.
Mail: Units 14 & 15, 1600 Steeles Avenue West
Concord, Ontario
L4K 4M2
Tel: (416) 736–5537
Fax: (416) 736–5793
Email: info@captus.com
Internet: www.captus.com

Library and Archives Canada Cataloguing in Publication

Dyer, Linda
Critical thinking for business students / Linda
Dyer. — 2nd ed.

Includes bibliographical references.
ISBN 978-1-55322-237-8

1. Business — Textbooks.
2. Critical thinking — Textbooks. I. Title.

BF441.D93 2011   650   C2010-907072-0

Canada ₧₧ We acknowledge the financial support of the Government of Canada through the Canada Book Fund for our publishing activities.

0 9 8 7 6
Printed in Canada

Contents

Midterm.

Preface

This handbook is intended for use as a supplemental text in undergraduate business courses. It teaches students to bring a critical perspective to their reading in various fields of business — evaluating authors' arguments, uncovering key assumptions, analyzing why certain texts are more persuasive than others, and practising related critical thinking skills. Each chapter contains the following elements: (i) expository text that discusses an aspect of critical thinking and shows why it is important to the process of evaluating ideas; (ii) worked examples of the critical thinking process applied to current, as well as classic, issues in business; (iii) brief sample texts that students can use to practise and develop their skills; (iv) exercises that encourage students to apply their skills and judgment to current business debates, and to read more widely in an area of their own interest.

I wish to thank Nicole Bérubé, an instructor who used the first edition of this book for many years. Nicole contributed insights and ideas as well as the text of some of the exercises in this edition. Her enthusiasm and wide-ranging interests were invaluable as we brainstormed ideas for new examples and updated resources. My colleague, Isabelle Dostaler, was also generous in her encouragement. Above all, I thank Charles Draimin, who read and re-read successive drafts, disputed my interpretations, offered constructive feedback, and provided unflagging support.

1

What Is
Critical
Thinking?

Critical thinking is an approach to reading, thinking, and learning that involves asking questions, examining our assumptions, and weighing the validity of arguments.

Sometimes questioning our beliefs about what we read comes naturally, but other times we may accept ideas and statements uncritically. Critical thinking can be developed as a frame of mind — a set of strategies that we will use as we determine whether or not to believe what we read or hear. In learning about critical thinking, we make these strategies explicit. If we can become aware of the activities of critical thinking, we will be able to use them consciously to think effectively and make intelligent decisions, both professionally and in our personal lives.

Critical thinkers are self-aware, curious, and independent. They introspect on their own thinking processes; they work at knowing their own biases and can name the strategies they are using when they make judgments (self-aware). They explore beneath the surface of issues by challenging ideas that seem to be obvious, trying out new approaches, and seeking new viewpoints to extend their knowledge (curious). They listen to the ideas of others and learn from them, but then they use that learning to develop their own informed opinions, to understand the full range of their options, and to make their own judgments (independent).

"You're so critical!"

When we use the word *critical* in our ordinary conversations with acquaintances, we often mean negative or judgmental. Actually, the word comes from the Greek word *kritikos*, which means to question, analyze, or make sense of something. This is the way we shall be using the term. Sometimes critical thinking will lead us to reject a conclusion; other times we will decide to accept an idea as valid. But in either case, we will have subjected the issue to careful thought. So critical thinkers are not necessarily negative; rather, they try to assess the truth about a given matter.

Critical thinking about business

Many people claim that this is the age of information. We are bombarded with information when we watch television programs, read newspapers, and explore the Internet. In recent times, information about the world of business often has appeared to hold centre stage. The dominant discourses are economic performance and the productivity of companies, global markets, financial investment, consumer awareness, changing career paths, and unemployment. This explosion of interest in business started in the mid-1980s. Two decades later, Simba Information, a company that does market research on the publishing industry, estimated that $2.2 billion worth of books about business were being sold globally each year. It is frequently suggested that the huge market for these books stems from business managers' struggles to compete effectively with rival companies. **Box 1.1** lists some classic best-selling business books in North America.

Box 1.1: Best-selling business books in North America

1. *Boom, Bust and Echo: Profiting from the Demographic Shift in the 21st Century* by David K. Foot with Daniel Stoffman (Stoddart, 2000).

   This book makes predictions about economic markets and social life in Canada based on demographics — the relative number of children, twenty-somethings, middle-aged, and elderly people in our society.

2. *Flow: The Psychology of Optimal Experience* by Mikhail Csikszentmihalyi (Harper Perennial, 1991).

   When we are fully engaged in a challenging activity that we truly love, we enter a state of "flow" in which we are most productive and happiest. With examples of surgeons, musicians, and many other case histories, the author's ideas speak to the pursuit of happiness at work.

3. *Freakonomics: A Rogue Economist Explores the Hidden Side of Everything* by Steven D. Levitt and Stephen J. Dubner (William Morrow, 2005).

   An unconventional scholar and a journalist apply economic theory to popular culture — their topics include drug-dealing, the socio-economics of naming children, and cheating among teachers and sumo wrestlers.

4. *Getting to Yes: Negotiating Agreement Without Giving In* by Roger Fisher, William Ury, and Bruce Patton (Penguin Books, 1991).

   The authors describe "principled negotiation" as a way to achieve agreement in the workplace. First published in 1981, it is now classic reading for sales representatives and business people who need to manage conflict.

(continued next page)

Box 1.1 (continued)

5. *Getting Things Done* by David Allen (Penguin, 2002).

   Allen, a management consultant and executive coach, provides insights about how to manage workflow and enhance productivity. The system has a devoted following, and "GTD" enthusiasts say that it has changed their lives.

6. *Good to Great: Why Some Companies Make the Leap...and Others Don't* by Jim Collins (Collins Business, 2001).

   Collins describes how a moderately successful company can become a great one by a careful focus of their strategies, employees, and corporate culture. This was probably the most successful business book in the first decade of the 2000s.

7. *In Search of Excellence: Lessons from America's Best-Run Companies* by Thomas J. Peters and Robert H. Waterman (Harper, 1982).

   The authors present case studies of successful companies and extracts eight principles for business success. The book was enormously influential and, although it has critics, many claim that its message has stood the test of time. One of the authors, Tom Peters, has become a management "guru".

8. *Now, Discover Your Strengths: How to Build Your Strengths and the Strengths of Every Person in Your Organization* by Marcus Buckingham and Donald O. Clifton (Free Press, 2001).

   Rather than trying to improve your weakness, the authors suggest, you should focus on your strengths to maximize your performance, enhance your confidence, and have a satisfying work life.

9. *Outliers: The Story of Success* by Malcolm Gladwell (Little, Brown & Company, 2008).

   The author explains that innate talent is not the most important cause of extraordinary success. Family, culture, and the "10,000 hour rule" are some of the less-obvious factors that contribute to a person's success. Gladwell is well known for translating academic theories into vivid, user-friendly anecdotes.

10. *Who Moved My Cheese? An Amazing Way to Deal with Change in Your Work and in Your Life* by Spencer Johnson and Kenneth Blanchard (Putnam, 1998).

    This 96-page business parable features two mice and two men who must learn to deal with organizational change. There are more than five million copies in print, and the book is frequently bought by managers for distribution to their employees.

In recent years, the market for trade books about business has declined. The 2001 collapse of the Texas energy-trading company Enron, the worldwide financial crisis of 2007–2010, and public reaction to similar business scandals may have contributed to the decreased interest in the writings of management gurus and retired executives. On the other hand, these events excited widespread debate about business ethics, the social responsibility of corporations, executive pay, and trust in the institutions of business. Online commentary on these matters enjoys unremitting growth. In addition, business magazines, seminars, workshops, and consultant reports, all contribute to the burgeoning business literature with which managers and other interested parties must cope.

The sheer volume of this information can be intimidating; critical thinking skills can play a vital role in helping us to sift through the multitude of ideas. Simply asking "Where have I heard this idea before?" helps us to deal with information overload. Critical thinkers recognize that the same idea can appear in radically different forms, and they search for commonalities among diverse texts. They discard the terminological chaff and conserve the enduring kernels of truth in the current understanding of how businesses work.

It is also said that this is the age of the expert. We count on experts to tell us how to look for a job, how to invest for our retirement, how to deal with difficult people at work, how to shop wisely. Our reliance on expertise extends beyond the boundaries of the workplace; we're given expert advice on nutrition, keeping fit, gardening, raising children, caring for aging parents, etc. The problem is that, all too often, experts disagree. Their ideas contradict one another. "For every theory dragging companies one way, there are two other theories dragging it in another," complain John Micklethwait and Adrian Wooldridge (1996: 16), two vocal critics of the business literature. How do we decide what to believe? If the business experts were infallible, there would be little need for critical thinking skills. But they are not. So we need to develop procedures we can use to assess the truth or validity of the differing ideas and conclusions the experts proffer.

Buyer beware

Many best-selling books written by business experts claim to deliver simple recipes for success that are based on a rich supply of anecdotes about successful executives and companies. They are often well written, entertaining, and optimistic in outlook. But *caveat emptor* — let the buyer beware. The ideas are not necessarily reliable, valid, or scientifically sound. The popularity of the books may say more about the effectiveness of the authors' and publishers' marketing techniques, or about the insecurity of the managers who buy the books, than about the worthiness of the books' contents. In the words of business scholar, Larry Cummings, best-selling business books are "frequently among the most dangerous because they are so well done (that is, well done in a marketing and journalistic sense), and therefore they are easily read and so believable. They are likely to influence the naive, those who consume them without critically evaluating their content" (Pierce & Newstrom, 1996: 22). A critical thinker does more than passively accept the ideas of others, even including the ideas of business experts.

As students of business, it is obvious that we need to think critically about the business discourse to improve our understanding of, and performance in, the world of commerce. Note, however, that critical thinking about business has a wider application. The values of business are permeating non-business spheres such as health care, politics, education, and the world of art and culture. The spread of business values is sometimes explicit, sometimes implicit, sometimes almost surreptitious. Government representatives, university administrators, hospital directors, police chiefs, boards of artistic and community organizations, all give voice to the pressure to revamp their activities to make them "run like a business", embracing values such as profitability, marketing, and competition. How valid is this generalization of business ideas to the not-for-profit sectors? What are the implications of extending the values of business into other spheres? It is important that we are able to ponder these issues and so to understand and evaluate the major role that the world of business plays in all aspects of our lives.

The sponge

Many writers about thinking skills use the idea of a "sponge" to demonstrate a procedure we should avoid when reading or listening to others. A sponge, whether it is the underwater marine animal or the pad lying beside the kitchen sink, simply sits there and soaks up liquid. A reader who acts like a sponge simply soaks up information. Of course, it is necessary to absorb knowledge about the world, particularly when you are learning about a new field. In your first marketing course, for example, you need to absorb the basics of marketing theory. Right now, you are "soaking up" some of the fundamentals of critical thinking. This is a necessary, though quite passive, exercise. It is preliminary to the next step — evaluating and judging critically ideas in marketing or other fields of business. This is the stage we must try to attain. Being a critical thinker means going beyond the level of being a passive sponge.

Dimensions of critical thinking

The critical thinking process can be divided into five major parts. First, critical thinking is purposeful — when we use these thinking strategies, we are trying to settle a problem, develop an answer to a question, or decide on appropriate action. It behooves us, therefore, to ensure that our thinking is directed at a significant and useful purpose and that we can state clearly the points at issue. This is the subject matter of the second chapter of this handbook, in which we focus on the **central claims** of business texts.

A second dimension looks at the quality of the data and reasons that are available to support claims. Are sufficient reasons provided? Is the information accurate? These and other questions that examine the **quality of the evidence** are presented in Chapter 3.

We also consider that claims and the evidence selected to support them are powerfully shaped by our basic assumptions or viewpoints. Can we identify the points of view that underlie the stated beliefs and evaluate their strengths and weaknesses? Can we turn our critical thinking focus onto our own **underlying assumptions and values**? Chapter 4 of the handbook looks at these notions.

Next, we pay special attention to inferences about cause and effect. In the field of business, many claims suggest prescriptions and formulae such as, "If you do X in your firm, then Y will be the result," or, "If employees are not given enough A, then they will become B." In Chapter 5, we will see that these are **causal claims**, and we will address the complex issue of judging the validity of causal inferences.

The fifth dimension to be considered here is the way in which ideas are expressed in order to persuade readers and listeners. As critical thinkers, we must consider carefully the way in which key concepts are presented, how contradictory evidence is managed, and in general, how words can sway our judgments. These ideas are presented under the broad heading, **Techniques of Persuasion**, in **Chapter 6**. The final chapter summarizes how the dimensions of critical thinking come together in writing a persuasive essay.

Consider an example

Let us now look at a brief text to which we might want to apply our critical thinking skills. There has been much concern recently about the underground economy, the notion that there are many transactions that occur among people who buy and sell goods and services "under the table" to avoid paying the applicable taxes. The following is a comment on the issue that we can evaluate critically:

> "I'd pay my taxes," says Richard, a Montreal landscape gardener and snow-removal contractor, "but they are too high and I get so little for them. I used to give receipts and accept cheques; I charged and paid GST and PST, and I declared all my income. People would offer to pay me cash under the table to avoid the GST and PST, but I said no. After a while, though, I asked myself what I was getting for all these taxes and decided that it really wasn't worth it. All these overpaid civil servants pushing paper until they get their fat, indexed pensions. All I get out of it is potholed roads, a failing health-care system, and giving welfare cheques to people who can but don't work. I have to scramble to get business and to satisfy difficult customers; and not even a good pension at the end. Anyway, I was losing customers to competitors who don't charge tax and probably don't declare their income either. I have food to buy for my family and credit card bills to pay. These things keep going up. I have no choice. I have to survive. If tax rates were lower, I'd pay my taxes and declare all my income. But the current set-up? No way!"

Richard's views are not exceptional. According to research by the Fraser Institute, an economic think tank, the underground economy now represents between 5 and 20 percent of GDP. It used to be smaller, but the expansion of small business and tax levels, and especially the introduction of the GST, over the past few decades have caused it to grow. Governments recognize this too. Today, lost taxes probably cost the federal and provincial governments something in the order of $30 to $40 billion. Governments' response is more stringent enforcement, as if this will solve the problem. But this misses the point. The answer is not heavy-handed enforcement of the tax law. It is expensive to hire government spies to chase down tax evaders. The answer, according to a director of the 70,000 member Canadian Taxpayers' Federation in Ottawa, is to reduce the tax burden to a level that people will judge to be fair. This will eliminate the incentive to cheat. High taxes force people to cheat. If taxes were lower, people would not resent complying.

As you read the text, several questions may occur to you as you decide whether or not the writer has made a good case for lowering taxes.

1. How relevant are Richard's household expenses to his argument that he should not pay taxes? In general, does the anecdote about Richard affect the persuasiveness of the author's conclusion?

2. Is tax reduction better than enforcement? Will compliance really increase if taxes are reduced?

3. If compliance does increase, will this make up for the loss caused by a lower tax rate?

4. What is the effect of phrases like "potholed roads", "fat, indexed pensions", and "government spies"?

5. Why does the author say that more stringent enforcement "misses the point"?

6. Who are the people who are likely to join the Canadian Taxpayers' Federation? What is the effect of noting that there are 70,000 members?

7. What do you think is the position of the author of this piece? In fact, who is the author and what is his/her background?

8. In your own opinion, what are the reasons that people evade taxes? Which, if any, of them are morally justified?

These are the types of questions a critical thinker raises. When you have applied your critical thinking skills to a piece like this, you may decide, in the end, to accept wholeheartedly the views of the author, to accept them cautiously and with specific reservations, to seek out further information before deciding one way or the other, or to reject the ideas outright. Whatever the outcome, you will have clearly defined reasons for your position.

Critical thinking and effective communication

Another important outcome of developing your critical thinking skills is that you can improve your own arguments when you write or speak. You will know how to state your views clearly and provide appropriate justification for them. You will be able to avoid fallacies in reasoning, explore your own underlying assumptions, and deal effectively with evidence that runs counter to your views. In general, you will develop further your appreciation for the use of *language*. Careful attention to words can make our writing not only clearer, but more persuasive. Throughout our discussion of critical thinking skills, we will find that they translate quite neatly into guidelines for effective communication.

2

Claims

The first thing we must do, if we are to evaluate an argument, is to identify the author's *claim*. A claim is the major conclusion of a piece of writing that the author is trying to persuade you to accept. It is pointless to criticize a thesis if you are unable to say clearly what the author's claim is.

Sometimes the central claim is explicitly stated and is easy to find. At other times, the job of finding the central claim is a greater challenge because it is implicit in the author's statements; that is, it is not stated outright. If the latter is true, you will have to state the claim in your own words. In a short article, the claim may appear at the very beginning of the piece. It sometimes appears in the title or as a headline of a newspaper article. The central claim may also be placed near the end of the article as a conclusion.

Certain words or phrases may indicate that the author is about to state a claim. They include words such as *therefore, thus, in summary, I believe that, clearly, in short, the data show that, as a result, in fact*, and synonyms of these words. If you are having trouble finding the claim, it may be helpful to look for these *cue words*, read the phrases that immediately follow them, then decide what seems to be the main idea of the article. It is important to ensure that your statement of the claim is *fair* — that you have not distorted the author's meaning. After taking the time to evaluate a claim in depth, you don't want the author to respond: "Actually, you've missed my point. That's not what I said!"

Most of the other statements in the article will be *evidence*, the examples and reasoning that are presented to support the claim, since it is normally on the basis of evidence that we decide whether or not to accept the claim. We will discuss evidence in some detail in another chapter. At this point, we simply note that a claim is not an example, a definition, or a statistic. It is usually a broader issue, addressed at a greater level of abstraction than the evidence. For example, let's say that you read a passage that reports an anecdote about the case of a company that took a retailer to court for selling counterfeit versions of their trademark products. In the same passage is the statistic that an estimated 39% of the software in Canadian computers was not legally purchased. Neither of these pieces of information is the claim; rather, the claim is the more general statement that pirated merchandise is a big problem for manufacturing firms. The anecdote and statistic are evidence provided in support of the claim.

Uncontested claims

Given our focus on questioning and evaluation, we might wonder whether there are any situations where we might accept a claim without examining the evidence. Should we accept *any* claim without challenge? In fact, shouldn't we probe and question *all* the information that authors present? Let us reiterate that critical thinking does not mean negative thinking. When we read or hear a claim, we may indeed decide to accept it as unproblematic. If we tried to question every single sentence that we read or heard, we would be paralyzed. Here are some conditions in which people may accept a claim without challenge, even if no evidence is provided in its support.

1. We usually do not contest claims that are consistent with our own experiences and observations, things that we have actually seen, heard, or touched: *The roads are congested with traffic between 4 and 6 pm*. Similarly, we accept claims that relate to subjective experiences: *I like the taste of black olives* or *Golf is my favourite sport*.

2. Some claims appear to be facts that are independent of interpretation — *Quebec is larger than Nova Scotia*. Events that happened are often not questioned: for example, when we read a newspaper report of a train accident or an announcement of a merger between two firms, we tend to accept this type of claim as true. These events are not uncommon and well within the realm of possibility.

3. Areas in which there is agreement among experts, or strongly supported general claims that are common sense, are often uncontested. Knowledgeable and intelligent people are in general agreement that *You cannot physically be in two places at one time*. Business scholars agree that *Frederick Taylor has often been called the father of modern management*.

4. Technical or mathematical claims are usually accepted without challenge. We do not question that debits equal credits in double-entry accounting or that a megabyte is 0.0009765625 of a gigabyte.

Of course, accepting something as unproblematic *now* does not mean that we must *always* continue to accept it as unproblematic. For example, even agreement among experts can be a transitory phenomenon. As new information arises, we are free to re-examine the situation and challenge claims that we no longer believe to be true. **Box 2.1** presents an example of a once-unproblematic claim that was re-examined in later years.

Contestable claims

When a claim does not fall into one of the categories described above, we need to question its truth or falsity using our critical thinking strategies. Authors may present claims that are not commonly accepted knowledge. For example, claims that *People who have excelled in the academic world*

Box 2.1: An uncontested claim becomes problematic

Henri Fayol, a French industrialist, developed a profile of the manager in 1916. "Managers," said Fayol, "plan, organize, coordinate, and control." Fayol's claim entered the general vocabulary of business and was accepted as unproblematic — his profile of managers was described in practically all introductory text books in business, and was routinely taught in business courses for undergraduates. There seemed to be general agreement among experts that this was an accurate characterization of managers.

Almost sixty years later, a challenge arose to Fayol's claim. Henry Mintzberg, a professor of management at McGill University, conducted a number of research studies in which he observed managers closely as they did their work. As a result, he published an article in the *Harvard Business Review* (1975) entitled, "The Manager's Job: Folklore and Fact".[1] The article begins, "If you ask managers what they do, they will most likely tell you that they plan, organize, coordinate, and control. Then watch what they do. Don't be surprised if you can't relate what you see to these words" (p. 163). Mintzberg proposed that Fayol's classic claim was merely myth or folklore. His aim in this article was to "break the reader away from Fayol's words and introduce a more supportable and useful description of managerial work" (p. 164). Rather than being a systematic and thoughtful planner, the manager has a job characterized by rapid pace, a variety of brief and discontinuous activities, and little time or inclination to reflect. Rather than planning broad strategies for the firm, based on aggregated, documented reports, managers prefer telephone calls, impromptu meetings, even hallway gossip.

Mintzberg made a new claim — that the manager's job was best described in a series of 10 roles. These included interpersonal roles (such as figurehead and leader), informational roles (including the collection and dissemination of information), and decisional roles (such as entrepreneur and disturbance handler).

Challenging Fayol's claim certainly rang bells with many managers. In a retrospective commentary, Mintzberg reports that a common reaction to his article was, "You make me feel so good. I thought all those other managers were planning, organizing, coordinating and controlling, while I was busy being interrupted, jumping from one issue to another, and trying to keep a lid on the chaos."

Note
1. H. Mintzberg, "The Manager's Job: Folklore and Fact", *Harvard Business Review*, March/April 1990, pp. 163–76. [The article first appeared in *Harvard Business Review*, July–August, 1975.]

---

make poor entrepreneurs or that *Having a mandatory retirement age decreases a country's productivity and economic progress* are contestable claims. Political commentaries and editorials in the newspaper are a rich source of contestable claims. It is important to note that readers and listeners find contestable claims to be much more interesting and significant than claims that can stand without challenge. Contestable claims often introduce new ideas that awaken curiosity and cause people to think about things in new ways. If everything we read was an unproblematic claim, it would be dull reading indeed.

On occasion, you may see a contestable claim presented as if it were a fact, as in **The fact is** *that close supervision is totally inappropriate in the modern workplace*; or in *There is **no doubt** that a sizeable increase in tuition is necessary to improve the quality of university education*. Simply labelling a claim as fact, however, or saying that it is beyond doubt, does not mean that it is an uncontested claim. Bosses, neophyte employees, and "old-hand" employees may have very different reactions to the claim about close supervision. Parents, students, professors, university administrators, and government officials may have varying opinions on the possible outcomes of a tuition increase. Neither claim, then, is independent of interpretation. Thus, unlike the examples in #2 above, both claims generally would be classified as contestable claims.

When making contestable claims, authors must provide evidence to justify their positions, and our job as critical thinkers is to examine and evaluate the justification. The quality of the reasoning and evidence (which will be covered in the next chapter) is what leads us to accept, or reject, contestable claims. Contestable claims cannot stand on their own. Without evidence, discussing contestable claims will rapidly degenerate into "my opinion against yours". In a related vein, we frequently hear the notion that "Everybody's opinion is of equal value" or "I have a right to my own opinion." Subjective opinions do have their place, of course, but little progress will be made in understanding the business world and how it works if we fail to see the crucial difference between simply stating that something is true and providing relevant and solid reasoning for our statements.

An example

Read the following passage and decide what the author's claim is.

"Self-praise is no praise at all." This was one of my grandmother's maxims. It is not socially acceptable to brag about yourself and your accomplishments, she said. Ladies and gentlemen do not boast.

But Grandma did not live in today's competitive work environment. Modesty is worse than useless at a job interview when dozens of my fellow-students are vying for the job I want. I'd be a fool not to tell the recruiter about the excellent paper I wrote about Activity-Based Costing, and how much I've learned about his company by surfing the Internet. And after I get the job, if I don't tell my boss how well my project is going, or the great skills I'm picking up at night school, who will? How will she know that I'm the one deserving of the big year-end bonus? Team-work is hot these days, and it's so easy to get lost in a crowd. I've got to let the right people know how many great ideas and long hours of work I contributed to the team effort. In short, it's a dog-eat-dog world, and if I want to get ahead, I've got to have the loudest bark.

You should have noted the cue words, *in short*, at the end of the passage. The claim is not stated explicitly, but the author's main point can be summarized as "Self-praise is necessary for career advancement." An alternative wording could be "Modesty is inappropriate in a competitive work environment," or "Bragging leads to success at work," or some similar formulation. It would not be appropriate to say that the claim was "It's a dog-eat-dog world," or "I've got to have the loudest bark," or even "Grandma was wrong." While these are colourful comments, they are not intelligible outside of the context of the passage, and none of them provides a good summary of the author's major point.

The rest of the paragraph contains the writer's reasoning and evidence presented in support of the claim.

Presenting claims

We have said that a good statement of the author's claim is the first step to evaluating it critically. When stating a claim, we try to present the essence of what the author is saying in an accurate and concise manner. Occasionally, we can find a sentence or phrase in the author's own words that is a good statement of his or her claim; more often, we must paraphrase and summarize elements of the text to state the claim clearly and efficiently.

While a claim is often stated as a sentence, especially when the text is short (like a newspaper article or the passage above), there are other ways of presenting claims. For longer texts, where a single sentence will not suffice, authors may provide a **list of important concepts** and a series of propositions about how these concepts are related. The claim may also be presented graphically as a diagram or drawing — a **concept map**. Concept maps are a compact way of summarizing complex material and can make the author's claims very memorable. A picture, the saying goes, is worth a thousand words. Concept maps may be simple boxes-and-arrows figures that highlight the main issues and show relationships. They may look like tree diagrams, geographical maps, or other creative images that summarize the author's main point. **Box 2.2** offers some tips in developing your own concept maps.

Box 2.2: Concept maps

The exercise of developing your own concept maps can help you to learn and remember the material you read for your courses. This is especially true when your concept maps contain images that are meaningful to you. In addition, concept maps can be an efficient and effective method of communicating the claims you make in your own reports to your readers.

(continued next page)

Box 2.2 (continued)

Pictures have become more and more central to people's understanding of the world around them. Beginning in the mid-nineteenth century, the then-new technology of the photograph led to an explosion of reproductions of pictures and images in posters, advertisements, books, newspapers and later, television. The historian Daniel Boorstin has labelled this phenomenon the "Graphic Revolution".[1] Some social observers believe that images are taking over from words as the primary medium of communication today.

We can conclude, then, that graphic representation of concepts and claims has become increasingly important for communication with the average reader. In fact, the cognitive processing needed to develop the concept map is an aid to our own understanding and memory.

Here are some tips to help you develop your own concept maps:

1. In making your concept map, start with a list of the main ideas to be represented. These may be headings or subheadings from the text. If headings are not provided, try to decide what words would be the most effective summary of each section of the text. It is important that you stick to single words or short phrases.

2. The structure of your map may be boxes and arrows, pictorial representations, timelines, a tree-and-branch organization, overlapping circles, or a variety of other formats. You do not need to pick a structure in advance, just let it develop naturally as you proceed with your thinking about the concepts and the relationships among them.

3. Remember that your concept map may be highly individual — its evolution depends on the images, symbols, and graphics that are most meaningful to you. You will find that certain conventions are intuitive — arrows, for example, usually denote cause-and-effect linkages; circles or other boundaries are used to group related ideas. You will develop your own conventions over time. Colour and shapes may be used judiciously: for instance, blue oval for advantages and red rectangle for disadvantages.

4. If you intend to use your concept map as an illustration in your own written report, make sure that it is well labelled and that the significance of the images you chose is clearly described in the text.

The strength of a concept map is its ability to summarize concisely large amounts of information. The concept map should never be more than one page. Having a few well-chosen words is much better than cluttering the map with excess words. Your goal is that a single glance will evoke ideas that may have been expressed in several pages of written information. This can be especially useful when you need to review material before an examination or oral presentation.

Note
1. D. Boorstin, *The Image* (New York: Harper & Row Publishers, 1961).

Writing effectively

Critical thinking about claims has implications for your own writing. Since a clear understanding of the claim is so important to readers, make sure that when you are the author you present your main ideas with clarity and emphasis. Put the claim near the beginning or end of your report, and use the cue words discussed above (e.g., *in conclusion, therefore, the data show that*) so that there can be no confusion as to what your claim is. The title of your text, and subheadings, where necessary, should make your logic transparent to the reader. Make your titles work for you. As a heading, *Section Three* is much less useful than *Executive Pay Should Be Public Knowledge.* In longer reports, you may find concept maps to be helpful in emphasizing your main points. Use pictures and other vivid images to make your claims clear and memorable for your readers.

EXERCISES

Exercise 2.1: Finding claims

Read each of the passages below and state the major claim being made by the author. What cues did you use to locate the claim? Is it a contestable claim?

1. So you want to be a chartered accountant? Get three months of work experience as a cashier, six months in the accounts department of a medium-sized merchandising company, and three months as an assistant to a field auditor. It is my view that before entering university, every young person should be asked to spend a year working "hands-on" in her or his chosen discipline. The pre-university year would give them the opportunity to take a realistic and logical decision that "this is what I really want to spend the rest of my life doing". No vicarious experience here, only hard facts and living knowledge. As a result, sitting in class listening to a professor lecture makes a whole lot more sense, because what is said is what you have experienced, and what gave you satisfaction. Both of my sons went that course; today, they are both on top of the heap in their respective professions. By effectively mixing the theory with the practical, you will be returning to the world of work as a graduate who can be productive almost immediately. And after all, productivity is what education is all about. It is a socializing phenomenon for preparing us to be good citizens — producing wealth, paying taxes, voting wisely, improving our society and living a good life.

2. Professor Michael Howe of Exeter University in England has done substantive research on excellent performance in sport and in the arts. As a result of his studies, he and his colleagues believe that the notion of innate ability — what we call talent — is a myth. Rather, success is determined by training, motivation and, above all, long hours of practice. Professor Howe studied expert swimmers, tennis

players, violinists, and so on, and found that thousands of hours of devoted practice were required for excellent performance, even among so-called "child prodigies". Many outstanding performers were not seen as particularly gifted as children, but training opportunities, encouragement, and hard work paid off for them over time. The myth of talent persists only because we do not normally observe the lengthy, gruelling practice sessions engaged in by most experts. Professor Howe's findings have important lessons for teachers, parents, and students alike.

3. Put six pots of jam on a table and offer people a $1 coupon towards buying jam. Some people will stop, try, and buy the jam. But then put 24 pots of jam on the table and offer the same $1 coupon. Many more people will stop, of course, but surprising to say, only one-tenth as many people will actually buy the jam. Why? Too much choice, according to the research of Sheena Igenyar, a professor at the Columbia Business School in New York. In everyday life in Western societies, people are faced with an overwhelming variety of choices. Whether you are choosing a box of cereal, a career, music to listen to, a travel destination, or even a mate, it may be helpful to realize that too much choice can be crippling. In fact, when limits are placed on our choices, these limits free us to act.

4. Bank employees used to have low-pressure, low-stress jobs, but with developments in telephone and electronic banking, all of that is changing. Workers at bank branches are no longer just tellers who carry out transactions; now, most routine transactions are done automatically. The job of the branch banker has become focused on learning about investment products, giving advice to customers, soliciting new business, and meeting sales targets to improve the bank's bottom line. And according to a study by the trade newspaper *Investment Executive*, bankers are reporting that these new duties are causing levels of pressure and job stress to rise.

5. Testing consumer products on animals must stop. Animal tests are not accurate; data from them cannot be extrapolated to human beings. There are enormous differences in metabolism and physiology among rats, rabbits, dogs, pigs, and human beings, so product tests on animals do not prove that the products are safe for human use. Every year 100,000 people die from taking prescription drugs that have been found to be safe in animal tests. Most cosmetic companies no longer conduct animal testing. Scientists can now create artificial skin, protein membranes, and even artificial brains to test irritancy or toxicity of substances. Companies no longer have to kill or maim defenceless animals to conduct their research. Corporations that continue to use animal tests must be persuaded — by concerned citizens and, ultimately, by government legislation — to find alternate means of testing their products.

Exercise 2.2: Contestable and unproblematic claims

*Review the following claims and decide whether they are **contestable** or **unproblematic**. Which of the contestable claims are true in your opinion? Which do you believe are false? Why do you think so?*

1. Employment equity legislation has made salary discrimination a thing of the past.
2. Children should be protected from commercial advertising.
3. A brain drain occurs when large numbers of skilled, college-educated, workers emigrate from a country.
4. The use of cross-functional teams increases the success rate of new product innovations.
5. There won't be enough money in the Canada Pension Plan to allow young people to have a comfortable retirement when they turn 65.
6. In 2010, a debt crisis in Greece caused turmoil in the European Union.
7. Rewards motivate employees.
8. In economics, equilibrium exists when supply equals demand.
9. The glass-ceiling syndrome is a primary reason why women leave large organizations and start their own businesses.
10. Pollution from industrial waste has been a leading factor in environmental degradation and decline.

Exercise 2.3

In this week's newspapers or business magazines, find two contestable claims and two uncontested claims that are relevant to the world of business.

You may want to look at the following publications both for this exercise and on a regular basis: Daily, you will find very informative the *Report on Business* in *The Globe and Mail* and the *Financial Post* section of the *National Post*; monthly, there is *Canadian Business* magazine. In addition, local city newspapers have business sections. Important U.S. business publications include the daily *Wall Street Journal* and the magazines, *Business Week*, *Forbes*, *Fast Company* and *Fortune*. The weekly business and current events magazine *The Economist*, published in Britain, is particularly good for international business news.

Exercise 2.4

Look at your readings for one of your other courses this term. Are there concept maps presented to illustrate any of the issues? What changes could you make to personalize these concept maps so that they become more meaningful and memorable for you? If no concept maps are presented, make a list of the important concepts in the text and develop your own concept map.

3

Evidence

We have defined a *claim* as the central idea that the author of a piece of writing is trying to persuade you to accept. An author who makes a claim usually offers reasons *why* you should accept it. *Evidence* is any statement that is a response to the question: Why is this true? It may consist of statistics, details of past events, anecdotes, written accounts, previously established claims, or other statements and reasoning that provide support for the claim. In the absence of evidence, a claim is merely an unsubstantiated opinion; the more contestable or controversial the claim, the more important that it be bolstered by solid evidence.

Finding the evidence

Evidence helps us to form judgments about claims. Just as it is crucial to identify the claim, we must locate the evidence before we can evaluate an argument. An *argument* is the combination of a claim and the evidence for it. Note that this differs from the common use of the word "argument" to mean "disagreement or contention". In a longer piece of writing, there will be several arguments — claims and evidence — that the author presents. Certain *cue words* indicate that the author is about to present a piece of evidence. Look out for phrases like *because, as a result, in the first place, in the second place, for example, in addition, given that, studies show, for the following reasons*, and similar phrases. Read the following passage, and locate the claim and evidence provided. The sentences are numbered to aid our analysis.

> Students today are more knowledgeable than they were a decade ago (1). In the first place, good early education plays an important role in this situation (2). Because of the prevalence of daycare, children leave home earlier, learning earlier to communicate with others and develop academic skills (3). For example, children in daycare are taught to read stories, write words and solve simple math problems even before they enter elementary school (4). In addition, teachers today are more highly educated than in the past (5). Most high school teachers hold at least a Bachelor's degree, and most university teachers have PhDs (6). At all levels, people receive training in teaching during their degree programs (7). Compared with the past, therefore, teaching is more effective nowadays (8). Finally, advances in high technology provide

students with a number of chances to expand their knowledge (9).
I read in the newspaper that more than 80% of Canadians have
access to the Internet at home (10). Nowadays, students can use
readily accessible, powerful Internet search engines to learn much
more information about their courses or other interests in a conve-
nient and efficient way (11).

Here, the central claim, *Students are more knowledgeable than they were
a decade ago*, is stated explicitly and appears both at the beginning and the
end of the passage. Why does the author think this? Several pieces of evidence are provided to answer our *Why is this true?* question. Notice the cue
words such as *in the first place, for example, in addition* and *finally*, which
precede the evidence. The evidence offered has to do with early learning
in daycare (sentences 2–4), the skills of teachers (sentences 5–8) and the
availability and power of Internet search engines (sentences 9–11).

Notice that each piece of evidence has to be explained — in fact, each
is treated like a subordinate claim which itself needs to be supported. The
broad, evidential statement about technology use, for example, is supported
by more detailed evidence about the prevalence of Internet access and its
use by students.

Quality of evidence

Of course, the mere presence of evidence is not automatic proof that
the claim is acceptable. Evidence may be strong and substantial or weak
and shaky. It is rare that we can be absolutely certain, beyond the shadow
of doubt, about the evidence for any claim. Our job becomes one of evaluating whether the supporting evidence is of high quality and makes the
claim highly probable, or whether it is of low quality, making the claim
highly dubious. There are a number of ways in which we can test the quality of the evidence.

Accuracy

The first and most important characteristic of good evidence is its
accuracy. Obviously, if you know that the information provided in justification is false, it undermines, if not negates, the claim. The problem is that
accuracy can be impossible to judge without an independent and infallible
source of information; usually we simply do not know whether the evidence
provided is accurate. We could set out to verify the information by doing
research of our own; more often we use *proxies* or other cues to decide
whether the information is accurate. One such cue is whether or not the
author makes other obvious errors. Even "trivial" errors, like grammar and
spelling mistakes, or inaccurate quotations, undermine confidence in the
author's reliability and make the argument less persuasive. Other cues that
suggest accuracy relate to the precision of the evidence and our judgment
about the source of the information (see below).

Precision

Good evidence is appropriately precise. If we hear that a mutual fund made 9.2% last year, we are more convinced by this precise number than if we were told that it did "quite well" or even "almost 10%". Saying that the turnout at a sports event was "rather low" is less effective than saying that only 63 people attended. Overuse of ambiguous and abstract words such as *a great deal, many, often, a high probability, few, usually*, and so on is indicative of low precision. Using numbers and providing direct quotations of what people actually said are the common ways of increasing the precision of our evidence. As we noted above, precision is sometimes used as a proxy for accuracy. Saying that 63 people attended suggests that we actually counted heads or ticket stubs, and that creates the impression of accuracy.

On the other hand, it is possible to be too precise. Appropriate levels of precision vary in different fields. It would be absurd for an accountant who is filling in his time sheet to say that he spent 17 hours, 9 minutes, and 34.6 seconds on a particular project, although someone in the field of athletics, say, a sprinter might measure his running speed in hundredths of a second. A manufacturer would not list a product weight as 8.4162 kilograms; that level of precision might, on the other hand, be quite appropriate for an experimental chemist. Over-precision, like under-precision, can detract from the credibility of our evidence. **Box 3.1** offers an explanation as to why numbers are associated with accuracy.

Box 3.1: Numbers and credibility

Isn't it odd that people are so impressed by numbers? Accountants, economists, psychologists, and their ilk take ordinary events and behaviours and translate them into numbers — and then their descriptions seem to acquire a special mystique. Just because activities are expressed in a quantitative language, people find them more convincing than when they are stated in simple prose.

Why such faith in the power of numbers? It is difficult to say, but part of the explanation may be that numbers are commonly associated with science. According to philosopher Abraham Kaplan, our excessive regard for numbers is a legacy of the nineteenth century, when advances in measurement led to great strides being made in the physical sciences.[1] Kaplan cites Lord Kelvin, who wrote: "When you can measure what you are speaking about, and express it in numbers, you know something about it; but when you cannot measure it, when you cannot express it in numbers, your knowledge is of a meagre and unsatisfactory kind." Quantitative measurement — numbers — in this view is the essence of scientific progress. Still today, as in the 19th century, science is generally believed to be the key to understanding the truth about our world, and thus the basis for improvements in human life and endeavours.

Note
1. A. Kaplan, *The Conduct of Inquiry* (New York: Harper & Row Publishers, Inc., 1963).

Sufficiency

To be persuasive, an author must present sufficient evidence to support a claim. In the field of business, it is unlikely that any claim can be substantiated by a single piece of data. If you had a single personal experience with a rude cashier last week, this incident alone would not be sufficient to support the claim that retail customer service has deteriorated markedly. Just how much evidence is sufficient, however, varies with the importance of the claim and the potential damage that would occur if the claim is incorrect. For instance, a teacher might ask three students whether her slides are readable from the back of the classroom. A team of researchers might sample 40 firms to determine what business practices make firms successful. Data from thousands of people would be necessary before politicians could claim that there must be a major change in laws governing health care.

When the evidence is not sufficient to support a claim, we say that the author is guilty of the *fallacy of hasty generalization*. A *fallacy* is defined as an "erroneous, but frequently persuasive, way of being led from a reason or circumstance to a conclusion." If we jump to a conclusion based on insufficient evidence, we are engaging in fallacious thinking.

Representativeness

Let us say that an author was making a claim about the reaction of Canadians to cutbacks in government services. The author teaches at a university, so he interviews students about their attitude to cutbacks and uses these interviews as the basis for his claim. Can this be considered good evidence? No. The problem is that university students tend to be younger than Canadians in general; they also may be more educated and have less disposable income. The evidence they provide is not *representative* of all Canadians. As a rule, the variety in the sources of evidence should match the variety in the population relevant to the claim. If an author is claiming that a certain company is abusive of employees and a terrible place to work, but the only people who consented to be interviewed were people who had quit or been fired, her data may not be a fair sample. It is not representative of those employees who have continued to work happily at the firm and her claim is undermined.

The *fallacy of hasty generalization* is also relevant to unrepresentative evidence. We should not be persuaded by evidence that does not come from a fair sample of information. For example, the accuracy of a forecast provided by a polling result depends on the sample that generates the result (see **Box 3.2**).

Authority

Typically, we don't have first-hand knowledge of the evidence when we write. Even experts have first-hand knowledge of only a small sample of experience. Every one relies on the experience of others. The question is, which others? When people have special training and professional credentials, or considerable experience in a particular area, we call them *authori-*

Box 3.2: Political polls and representativeness

Can political polling predict election results? Often it can. Political polls are interesting for another reason — there is an immediate and definitive confirmation of the prediction. Polling, therefore, is one of the few areas in which researchers can determine just how representative their evidence is. If the information collected by the pollsters is drawn from an unrepresentative sample of the population, the poll results will be misleading.

A classic case occurred during the U.S. presidential election of 1936. The editors at the *Literary Digest* (a news magazine) mailed 10 million postcards to voters asking them who they planned to vote for — Alf Landon or Franklin Roosevelt. Of the two million responses they received, the votes were overwhelmingly in favour of Landon. A fortnight later, Roosevelt won by the largest landslide in American history. Why had the poll been so misleading? The *Digest* developed its mailing list using telephone directories and lists of car owners. Unfortunately, this created a sample with a bias in favour of the wealthy; only richer people could afford cars and telephones in those days. Poorer people were more likely to vote for Roosevelt as his political platform stressed jobs for the unemployed.

In the same election, another poll predicted the result accurately. This poll was an early success of George Gallup,[1] who had used a more representative sample. Yet even the famous Gallup polls have proved erroneous; their poll in 1948 predicted that Thomas Dewey would win the presidential election over Harry Truman. One of the explanations for their failure was that their sampling procedure under-represented people who lived in cities and over-represented people from rural areas. Since it was largely city people who favoured Truman, the number of their votes was under-estimated by Gallup's poll.

Note
1. To learn more about the history of the Gallup polls, see <http://www.gallup.com/corporate/1357/corporate-history.aspx>.

---

ties and pay close attention to the evidence they provide. When writers cite business scholars and experienced business people, this lends authority to their arguments. The currency of the source is important. Apart from the classics in any subject, current writing is usually more authoritative than older sources, particularly in rapidly changing fields where new discoveries are important.

In addition, authority is context-dependent. A legal argument needs, first and foremost, authoritative legal sources, while scientific writing will cite the evidence produced by other scientists. On the other hand, we should be less persuaded when a film star endorses a particular diet regime or a sports hero is used to convince us of the usefulness of buying car insurance; in both cases, the endorsers are providing evidence outside their area of expertise. This is termed the *fallacy of false appeal to authority*, which we commit when we accept the testimony of someone who has no expertise in the relevant area. Sadly, advertisers know how easy it is for us to succumb to this fallacy!

Another fallacy that is related to the source of the evidence is the fallacy of *argumentum ad populum* which, loosely translated, means "appeal to the people". The mere fact that many people accept a belief is not in itself evidence that the belief is correct. This fallacy has also been called the *bandwagon effect*. If a manufacturing manager claims that adopting a "Six Sigma" program would be good for the company just because "everybody is on the Web these days", he may be falling prey to the fallacy of *argumentum ad populum*, especially if he has no independent basis for the belief apart from the knowledge that others are doing it. He is also presuming, perhaps erroneously, that other firms exercised good judgment when they decided to adopt the Six Sigma program.

Clarity of expression

The significance of the evidence should be clearly stated. A common failing is that authors provide information as evidence, but they are not explicit about what this information signifies. Often it is the use of tables, figures, charts, or graphs that creates this problem. In our discussion of precision above, we noted that quantitative data can be quite persuasive. Data must always, however, be interpreted for the reader. Numbers do not speak for themselves. Consider the following table:

Firm	Grievance rate	Absence rate	Firm performance
1	8.2	3.97	2.7
2	3.2	3.00	6.1
3	6.5	2.71	4.6
4	7.4	2.38	3.3
5	2.6	1.84	4.9

Quite precise, but what does it mean? The author should summarize the table, explaining the meaning of the numbers and telling us clearly that he interprets the numbers as showing that unhappy employees, defined as those who file grievances and are absent relatively often, undermine the performance of the firm. Once the evidence is expressed with clarity, the table begins to take on some meaning, and we can then see how it might bolster the author's claim that good people-management improves business success. So, too, should direct quotations be clearly interpreted when they are offered in evidence.

A sample analysis

Let us look again at the passage above that claims that students today are more knowledgeable than they were in the past. Here is a sample response that evaluates the quality of the evidence presented and discusses whether, on the whole, the reader is persuaded by the argument.

Accuracy I have independent information that suggests that some aspects of the data are accurate. For one thing, I have heard on TV about government initiatives to make daycare more affordable for the increasingly large number of dual-career couples and single parents, so perhaps that means that more children are indeed attending daycare compared with 10 years ago. On the other hand, I have no means of judging the accuracy of the statements about what kids actually learn in daycare. Second, my uncle is a teacher, and a few years ago he went back to school to do a graduate diploma so that he could continue in his career. In general, it is well known that teachers have increasingly been required to seek higher education in order to obtain the positions they want. However, I am unable to evaluate the accuracy of the comment that teachers are trained in teaching more frequently than they used to be 10 years ago. And as far as computers go, there is no question in my mind that nowadays more people have computers and Internet connections; the falling prices and conversations with my friends and acquaintances make this obvious to me. In summary, my evaluation of accuracy is mixed. I need to find other clues before I'd be willing to accept the evidence as accurate in its entirety.

Precision The information is fairly general. The author talks about *the prevalence of daycare*. It would have been more convincing if I had been given a percentage of children in daycare now, compared with a percentage 10 years ago. Also, *most high school teachers* is not precise. Even the statistic that *more than 80% of Canadians have access to the Internet at home* should have been more precise. There are no specific quotes presented. To my mind, the low precision detracts from the argument. In fact, if more precise numbers had been given throughout, it might have encouraged me to believe that the author had done careful research, which would create a more positive evaluation of *accuracy* as well.

Sufficiency Three different pieces of evidence are presented. For a text of this length, this might be deemed sufficient, especially since the claim does not have important policy implications. In other words, the truth or falsity of the claim may make for lively Sunday dinner conversations, but it is unlikely to affect education policies or practices. So I am satisfied that three pieces of evidence are sufficient for this claim.

Representativeness The types of evidence are quite varied, including evidence about how people learn in early childhood as well as when they are older students. Evidence includes both the content of knowledge (the three Rs, Internet information and teachers' knowledge of their disciplines) and the process of gaining knowledge (teaching skills, the convenience and efficiency of the Internet). I might have expected to see some comparison of the school curricula then and now, but in general I am moderately satisfied with the diversity, or representativeness, of this evidence.

Authority I don't know who the author of this piece is, or what are his or her qualifications and expertise. Nor are any other authorities actually mentioned in the text. At one point, the author says that he or she *read in the newspaper* a particular bit of evidence, but does not even mention which newspaper it was. It might have been a respected publication like *The Globe and Mail* or it might have been a neighbourhood weekly where the contributors may be less careful of their facts. It might even have been a computer news publication that might be biased in favour of overstating the percent of computer ownership. The absence of any controlled scientific research detracts from the authority. The opinions of an experienced teacher might also have helped, but as it stands, the text has very low authority. If there had been more authoritative information, it might also have helped to convince me that the evidence is *accurate*.

Clarity of expression The text is easy to read because the reasons are quite clearly expressed. The points are laid out in simple sentences with the claim explicitly stated at the beginning and the evidence summarized at the end.

Overall, my reaction to this argument is mixed. While the evidence appears to be sufficient, representative, and clearly expressed, I remain uncertain about the accuracy, especially since the precision and authority are so weak. The author needs to do more work if she or he is to convince me that I should accept the claim based on this evidence.

Other objections

As you read the analysis above, you may have objected to yet another aspect of the argument. If you believe that children learn just as much at home with a parent or nanny as they learn in a daycare, or that however early kids are taught, by eight years of age there is no difference in knowledge, then the increasing use of daycare will not be deemed *relevant* to the claim. If you think that most of the time on the Internet is spent playing online games, downloading movies, or networking with friends, then you will not accept that widespread use of technology is *relevant* to increased knowledge among students. If you believe that people's greater expertise is unrelated to how well they can communicate with lay-persons, then the advanced degrees of today's teachers will not be seen as *relevant*. All these issues of relevance are related to your **underlying assumptions**, which is the topic of the next chapter.

Effective writing

When we study an issue and report our findings, we should present our argument in the form of a claim and supporting evidence. For complex arguments, each piece of evidence may be treated in turn as if it were a claim, and further, more detailed evidence is presented in explanation. Provide your readers with the wherewithal to determine whether your evidence is sound. Citing the sources of your evidence allows your readers to judge the *authority*, and so the *accuracy* of the information. (Of course, we also cite the sources because it is essential, when we use other people's ideas, to give credit where credit is due). Your readers will judge the authority of your views as a writer, too, since the selection of inappropriate or inaccurate sources reflects on the writer's judgment. Remember that one of the purposes of writing is to join the authority chain as well, if only in the eyes of the reader. If the claim is controversial, you must recognize this and not assume that one piece of evidence is *sufficient*. As well, note that when more than one authority must be cited, the selection of experts must be *representative*. Even if the readers cannot themselves describe the range of serious views, they can see quickly enough whether your selection of evidence has the appearance of being fair. Recall, too, that appropriate *precision* and *clear* statements of the significance of your evidence are crucial. Avoid the over-use of abstract, ambiguous words in your writing.

EXERCISES

Exercise 3.1: Evaluate the evidence
Read the passage below and state the major claim that is being made. Identify and evaluate the evidence that is presented for the claim, discussing its accuracy, sufficiency, precision, representativeness, authority, and clarity of expression.

Bottled water is a $15 billion business in North America, according to an article by the newspaper *The Globe and Mail*, with a per capita consumption of about 20 gallons. Sales are dropping, however, because of an increasing wave of criticism by environmentalists.

A report by the U.S. Natural Resources Defense Council (NRDC) revealed that 25% of bottled water comes from municipal sources. Since bottlers are not required to list the source on the bottle, many people would be surprised to learn that they are drinking glorified tap water, purchased at high prices. Some sources estimate that the price of bottled water is in fact as high as the price of gasoline. Although some consumers may be willing to pay high prices for higher safety, the NRDC warns that while regulations are in place to safeguard bottled water, these are not applied universally and bottlers are not required to let consumers know that their product may be contaminated. The NRDC tested more than 100 brands of bottled water and found evidence of contamination in single samples of at least a third of the brands the agency tested.

Aside from the water itself, the plastic containers are sources of pollution and may contribute to contaminating the water they contain. Dr. Todd Jarvis, the associate director of the Institute for Water and Watersheds at Oregon State University, calculated that 72 billion gallons of water were needed to produce the plastic bottles used to store bottled water worldwide in a single year. The Container Recycling Institute estimates that less than 20% of these containers are recycled. The environmental cost of bottled water is thus high, especially when considering the carbon emissions cost of transporting bottled water over long distances.

Exercise 3.2: Evaluate the evidence

Read the passage below and state the major claim that is being made. Identify and evaluate the evidence that is presented for the claim, discussing its accuracy, sufficiency, precision, representativeness, authority, and clarity of expression.

Question: Who is best placed to evaluate managers? Answer: Anybody who has interactions with them. Tradition has it that the person who is one step above the manager in the organization's hierarchy is the prime evaluator, but it is clear that anyone who interacts with the manager on the job can provide valuable feedback about the manager's performance — this may include peers, subordinates, and even customers and suppliers.

Managers nowadays often work in teams, collaborating and coordinating their efforts with co-workers in other divisions or departments. Furthermore, today's managers supervise workers who are more educated and technically skilled than was the norm 25 years ago. These "knowledge workers", who often know more than the managers themselves about particular tasks, need to be stimulated and inspired, rather than simply told what to do.

In addition to supervising a new breed of worker, managers today operate in a business environment that is characterized by rapid and unpredictable change. They must keep interacting with suppliers, customers, and other people outside the organization, all of whom can provide valuable information that will keep the firm competitive.

What can we demand of managers, then? The flexibility to adapt to changing technologies and market conditions; the ability to involve subordinates in decision making so as to employ their talents most fully; and skill at articulating an inspiring vision that energizes subordinates and stimulates them to maximal performance. The managers' peers, subordinates, suppliers, and customers are in an excellent position to assess these characteristics in an accurate and fair manner. The system of performance evaluation that elicits feedback from this variety of sources is called 360-degree feedback; this system has been deemed one of the most important recent advances in human resources by management scholars, consultants, and business executives alike. Companies like Petro-Canada, Coca-Cola, DuPont, and Disney Corporation have all used variants of the 360-degree technique.

Self-evaluation is also part of 360-degree assessment. If the manager can say, for example, "I feel that my skills at generating new business are weak, and my peers and subordinates agree with me," this is the first step in the development process. Having such issues emerge in a self-evaluation also puts the responsibility on the boss to provide training or support for the managers. It has been the experience of many companies that even if the ultimate responsibility for performance evaluation stays with the boss, 360-degree evaluation has an appreciable positive impact on managers' skills, motivation, and performance.

Exercise 3.3: Evaluate the evidence

Read the passage below and state the major claim that is being made. Identify and evaluate the evidence that is presented for the claim, discussing its accuracy, sufficiency, precision, representativeness, authority, and clarity of expression.

Employee job satisfaction is bad for business. According to Professor Jing Zhou at the Jones Graduate School of Business at Rice University, grumpy employees are more productive and recent empirical data does not support the notion that job satisfaction leads to improved productivity. Happy and co-operative employees, Professor Zhou points out, are productive in stable business environments where routine tasks predominate. However, modern business environments are volatile and require a great deal of day-to-day adjustments. Happy people get in a rut and don't think well enough to handle complex tasks and respond to highly competitive environments.

Professor Zhou's 2007 survey of 149 employees revealed that the most dissatisfied employees were also the most creative. It appears that dissatisfaction engages the process of creativity as people try to find a way to relieve their dissatisfaction. On the other hand, when people are happy, they become complacent, and this stifles creativity. This is because happy people do not see problems and, consequently, make no effort to solve them. Unfortunately, most organizations tend to reward employees who agree with organizational management, the "yes" men and women. On the other hand, disgruntled employees are reprimanded or ignored. When this happens, dissatisfied employees tend to react by pretending nothing is wrong, effectively stifling their ability to solve organizational problems.

Does this mean that managers should foster discontent among employees? The answer is not that simple, says Professor Zhou. Rather, managers should focus on problems to be solved, encourage people to identify issues and voice their opinions. It is also important to understand that to harness the creative advantages of dissatisfied employees, organizations must retain them. This is counter-intuitive since dissatisfied employees are often encouraged to leave, or leave without encouragement. Therefore, managers should create a context where employees would find it difficult to leave the organization. Such conditions would encourage employees to work towards improving the organization since the cost of leaving the organization would be prohibitive.

Professor Zhou asserts that her rigorous research provides strong evidence that it's time to turn conventional wisdom on its head and harness the creative zeal of discontented employees.

Exercise 3.4: Evaluate the evidence in the recent business news

*Using this week's business news, find an article that proposes a **contestable claim**. State the claim in one or two sentences, paraphrasing it for clarity, if necessary. What evidence is presented for the claim? Evaluate the evidence in terms of accuracy, sufficiency, precision, representativeness, authority, and clarity of expression.*

Exercise 3.5: Collecting evidence

Here is a list of claims. In your opinion, are they more likely to be true, or false? If you had to collect evidence from various sources to support or refute these claims, where would you look? Think of the qualities of good evidence to ensure that you have the information to build the best possible case for your viewpoint. For each claim, provide a list of potential sources of evidence.

Choose one of the claims and follow up on the sources of evidence that you listed. Evaluate the evidence you find in terms of its precision, sufficiency, representativeness and authority.

1. Electronic commerce has seen extraordinary growth in the past decade.

2. The price of university textbooks outstrips their usefulness.

3. Having a pet does wonders for one's physical and psychological health, particularly for elderly people who live alone.

4. Women's management styles are different from men's.

5. Increasingly, young Canadians find that they cannot afford to leave home and set up their own households.

4

Underlying
Assumptions

Consider the following case:

> Mammon Corporation spent over two million dollars on management consultants during the years 2002–2004. Much of the money was spent on business process re-engineering; several business units were eliminated and hundreds of employees lost their jobs through downsizing. A journalist writing about Mammon's performance claimed that the money spent on the consulting engagements had been wasted. Why? In reviewing the firm's annual report, she noted that profits reported in 2005 were no higher than they had been in the previous three years.

If we translate this case into our critical thinking terms, we can state it this way:

> Claim: Mammon Corporation wasted money on re-engineering consultants.
>
> Evidence: Over two million dollars was spent, but profitability has stayed about the same.

Are we persuaded by the journalist's claim that the money was wasted? Only if we agree that the 2005 profitability figures are *relevant* to the claim. In other words, do we agree that the 2005 profits *should count as evidence* that money was wasted? The general principle that connects the claim to the evidence is, "If money is spent to improve a business, but profits do not go up the next year, the money has been wasted." This principle is an *underlying assumption*. It is a logical link that fills the gap between the evidence and the claim.

Some readers may decide that the journalist's underlying assumption is sound. Re-engineering is a painful and costly process, and if the payoff for the firm is minimal, then indeed the money was wasted. Other readers may question the assumption. Perhaps there *was* a significant improvement in performance, but economic conditions in the industry were much worse in 2005. If Mammon had not engaged in re-engineering, it might be in receivership today. Keeping profits from falling is excellent performance under such conditions! Perhaps the money spent on financial packages for departing employees reduced profits this year, but since this was a one-time extraordinary charge, we might expect that future profits will be much higher if the re-engineering decision were correct.

As critical thinkers, we must find and state the author's underlying assumptions. What are the suppositions upon which the argument is based? What must we believe if we are to see the evidence as relevant to the claim being made? Subjecting underlying assumptions to careful scrutiny is an important step in the critique of a text. Even when the evidence is of good quality — accurate, precise, clearly expressed, authoritative, sufficient, and representative, the argument is not acceptable if the underlying assumptions are questionable.

Why are they "underlying"?

We said earlier that underlying assumptions are usually found in the "gap" that separates claims and evidence. But why does this gap exist? Shouldn't authors be more careful to show exactly why every piece of evidence is relevant to the claim? Why are underlying assumptions generally *implicit* instead of *explicit*? In other words, why are assumptions "underlying"? The answer is that once a person's assumptions about a certain topic are formed, they are the foundation of everything she thinks, says, and does on that topic. They are deeply ingrained and taken for granted. It is quite rare that she would think consciously about the assumption. It simply becomes part of her tacit belief system — as natural as walking and breathing. This taken-for-grantedness of our assumptions is true for all of us.

For example, a common assumption in our society is that children should learn how to read and write. Basic education is valued. Even when we complain about the school system, we do not wonder whether or not literacy is a good thing — its value is taken for granted. This assumption is the foundation of many debates about child labour. An activist might claim that consumers should boycott factory goods like carpets and shoes that come from the labour of children in certain Third World countries. His or her evidence is, "Children work long hours in these factories, and have neither the time nor the freedom to go to school — they remain illiterate." The activist does not usually add, "And being literate is a good thing." This underlying assumption is taken for granted by both the activist and his readers or listeners.

So there is nothing wrong, really, with having unstated underlying assumptions. Authors who leave them out are not necessarily hiding them or trying to fool us. They are just taking them for granted as we all do. The only problem is that different people have different assumptions, reflecting different values. Other assumptions represent matters of fact — beliefs about reality — and they may be quite wrong or, at least, debatable. (We will return to value and reality assumptions in a later section). So uncovering assumptions and making them explicit is an important step in evaluating any argument. The process allows us to judge whether the evidence is relevant or appropriate support for the claim, and so, whether we should accept the claim. Needless to say, we tend to pay most attention to an author's underlying assumptions when they conflict with our own point of view! It is an important discipline, however, to examine assumptions explicitly even when we agree with the author's claim.

How to find underlying assumptions

In essence, we find underlying assumptions by looking at what people write, then making guesses about what they must believe in order to have written that. We look for the gap between the evidence and the claim by asking: *What must be true if the claim is to follow from this evidence? What general principle might link this particular claim to this particular evidence?* Sometimes it is useful to put oneself in the role of the writer. *What beliefs might I expect from this type of person?* For example, if you were role-playing a CEO (downsized worker, consultant, shareholder), what would you think about the evidence about consultants being a waste of money for Mammon Corporation? Other times, it is useful to be a devil's advocate: *Could someone believe this evidence and still disagree with the claim? Why?*

Sometimes finding underlying assumptions is easy because the gap between evidence and claim is a small one. At other times, however, the gap is large and pinning down the assumptions is quite difficult. When an author is very knowledgeable about a complex topic, she may leave large gaps in her logical connections between claims and evidence. She may be taking it for granted that her readers are also very familiar with the topic. Furthermore, when a person feels strongly about a claim, his emotions may overtake the logical presentation of his ideas and reasoning, and large gaps between evidence and claim may result.

Consider the following example:

> I was listening to a radio talk show that was dealing with the topic of the North American Free Trade Agreement, trying to assess the aggregate benefits and costs to Canadians in the 10 years since NAFTA was signed in 1989. One participant maintained that free trade had proved to be a very bad idea. He described an experience that, in his view, demonstrated conclusively the problems of free trade. Here's the evidence he presented (summarized and paraphrased):
>
> > My favourite shoes have always been Clark's Wallabees. You know Clark's — the British shoe company. I've worn those shoes all my life; they are so comfortable. Some years ago, however, they disappeared from the shelves. I couldn't find them anywhere. Finally, a shoe store offered to order them specially for me. But when the shoes arrived, I could see right away that something was wrong. The soles were an odd, pale colour and they looked really awful. They didn't fit properly, and to add insult to injury, they cost more than I had ever paid for a pair of Wallabees in the past. I looked inside under the

tongue to check the size. The size was correct, but it also said: Made in China! There, in a nutshell, is the problem with free trade!

Briefly put, we have

Claim: Free trade is a bad idea

Evidence: The Chinese-made shoes had the wrong colour, the wrong fit, and were very expensive.

What, we may justifiably ask, does this disappointing shoe order have to do with free trade? Why is this evidence relevant to his claim? From his tone, it seemed so clear to him that this evidence was telling! If it is not so obvious to you, you are not alone. It requires some thought to make his underlying assumptions explicit. Here is an interpretation of what he *might* have said had he been pressed to explain the link between the evidence and his claim:

1. Free trade has opened the floodgates to products made in less-developed countries.

2. Because labour is cheap in less-developed countries like China, the cost of manufacturing products there is low.

3. The quality of these products is also very low; for example, many shoes made in the less-developed countries are of poor quality.

4. People in Canada are sensitive to price and like the opportunity to buy cheap shoes.

5. Traditional, high-quality shoe manufacturers cannot compete at these prices. They either go out of business or start making their shoes in the less-developed countries as well, in which case the shoes are lower in quality.

Therefore, the argument is

My new Wallabees are low-quality because of free trade.

Assumptions #1, 2, 4, and 5 seem necessary to explain why Wallabees are now made in China. Most economists would agree that these assumptions are reasonable. Assumption #3 seems necessary to explain why he does not like the quality of his new Wallabees. Note that complex arguments often conceal *multiple* underlying assumptions.

The next stage for the critical thinker is evaluating these underlying assumptions. Is #3 an accurate assumption? This is debatable. His performance could just be subjective, and other people might find the new shoes look and fit just fine. Moreover, assumptions #1, 2, 4, and 5 seem inconsistent with his statement that the shoes are expensive. How could the shoes from less-developed countries have undermined the market for high quality shoes if they were not cheaper? In his price comparison, has he taken inflation into account? Is he taking into account the fact that perhaps he is being charged more for this special order? In sum, we will need some more careful explanations before we accept the story of the shoes as relevant evidence for the undesirability of free trade.

Reconstructing and evaluating underlying assumptions sometimes requires that we *learn more* about issues and a variety of points of view. Knowledge of economics helps us to flesh out the assumptions being made about free trade. As you continue to take courses in business, your knowledge base will increase, which will allow you to detect underlying assumptions more easily, and to be able to judge their worth.

Reality assumptions

There are two major types of assumptions, *reality assumptions* and *value assumptions*. Reality assumptions are our beliefs about what events have taken place, what exists, or how things work in the world. In other words, they are our beliefs about reality, the way things really are. Our first-hand experiences, our conversations with others, the things we read or see on television — all these shape our beliefs. In particular, when we have considerable experience that is consistent with a given belief, the belief becomes *taken for granted*. The example given in the section above is based on reality assumptions about the economics of free trade. We can guess that the man on the radio talk show had developed these ideas about how international trade works through reading, conversation, and his experiences as a consumer over many years.

Another reality assumption was encountered in the previous chapter in the text that claimed that students are more knowledgeable now than they used to be. One piece of evidence offered was that teachers have more advanced degrees today than was the case in the past. The evidence is relevant only on condition that (a) People with advanced degrees have more and better quality knowledge; and (b) they can pass this better knowledge base on to students effectively. These two underlying assumptions describe the author's taken-for-granted beliefs about what makes a teacher effective. **Box 4.1** presents another example of reality assumptions in organizations.

Challenging reality assumptions

Once an author's reality assumptions are made explicit, the next step is to evaluate their accuracy. As mentioned above, this usually consists of critiquing the quality of the assumptions. In the free trade example, we could argue that the assumptions were logically inconsistent, and did not take into account important economic variables such as inflation. Another way of challenging reality assumptions is to provide data that would show that the assumption is incorrect. In the "knowledgeable students" example, we might show that people who have developed great expertise often

Box 4.1: Reality assumptions about employees

It's human nature for people to do as little work as they can get away with; the average employee is indolent, unambitious and dislikes responsibility. Employees must be supervised closely or they will not work to fulfill organizational goals. If, however, they are given enough money, they will generally accept direction and will be productive.

These assumptions about employees are the basis of the motivational policies, practices, and programs of many firms. Douglas McGregor, a management scholar, coined the term **Theory X** to label this set of beliefs. McGregor proposed that Theory X assumptions were an inadequate description of human motivation. He made an alternative set of propositions, which he called **Theory Y**: *People are not passive or lazy by nature. They only become so because that is how they are treated in organizations. The capacity for assuming responsibility and using creativity and imagination to further organizational goals does exist in employees. It is up to managers to create the organizational conditions that will release employees' potential.*[1]

McGregor first formulated Theory X and Theory Y over 40 years ago. In those days, Theory X, with its focus on external control of behaviour, was the conventional view. McGregor described Theory Y, which relied on self-control and self-direction, as a bold and innovative proposal.

Arguably, management today is still dominated by Theory X reality assumptions. For example, when managers install systems to monitor employees' use of the Internet during working hours, they are acting on Theory X assumptions. They may believe that without control employees will spend company time in frivolous surfing of the net. Firms that hire roving, "mystery" customers to check up on the service provided by their sales representatives are reflecting a Theory X assumption that, without this surveillance, employees would be lackadaisical or rude. It is true that we do hear a lot about empowerment and self-managing teams nowadays. These are practices that are consistent with a Theory Y framework. But we have to ask ourselves whether these terms represent a true change in management assumptions — one often has the impression that managers are just paying lip service to these ideas; all the while their actual behaviour is thoroughly "X".

McGregor anticipated that progress toward the goal of Theory Y would be slow and difficult. After generations of Theory X management, it was unlikely that employees or managers could shift to a Theory Y framework overnight. Clearly, many firms are taking steps in the direction of Theory Y, but it is equally clear that Theory X continues to be the predominant reality assumption among managers today.

Note
1. D. McGregor, "The Human Side of Enterprise", *Management Review*, November 1957, pp. 41–49.

find it *harder* to communicate their knowledge to lay people, since they have forgotten what it was like to be so naive. We might present data to show that only a small percentage of graduate programs offer serious training in how to teach. *In general, to challenge reality assumptions, we must present information showing that the author's notions of reality and how the world works are debatable or just plain wrong.*

Value assumptions

Values are our ideals, our standards of right and wrong, the way things ought to be. We can recognize them through the use of words like *ought, should, desirable, unacceptable,* and so on: "You should keep your promises," "Teachers ought to treat students fairly," or "Co-operative work is desirable." Often, values are learned early in childhood from our parents, teachers, classmates, or through religion; other values are adopted later on, in our adult lives. Some values are very commonly held: being honest, helping those less fortunate than ourselves, having the freedom to express our views as citizens are widely seen as good things. In the world of business, there are many specific values that embody our ideas of what is right and wrong. Bosses *ought* to be helpful and encouraging to their subordinates. They *ought not* to use their power to gain sexual favours. Large, successful companies *should* exhibit social responsibility by making donations to community, cultural, or sporting events, and by not polluting the environment. Businesses *should* adopt strategies that allow them to stay competitive. **Box 4.2** illustrates how "competitiveness" is part of our everyday life.

Although there is widespread agreement about some values in our society, *value conflicts* are also quite common. Because I value honesty, I might feel I should tell the boss about my co-worker who confessed to me that he'd lied about his qualifications for the job. You might disagree, feeling that I shouldn't tell the boss, since you value loyalty to one's peer group. Sometimes these value conflicts happen within the individual. When approached by a beggar, we may feel torn between compassion and the feeling that people ought to work for their living. Values may be *ranked* differently by different people. Some people feel much more strongly about corporate social responsibility or sexual harassment, for example, than others do.

Challenging value assumptions

Value conflicts and differential value rankings are reasons for disagreements about the relevance of the evidence presented for a claim. In the following example, three business students are discussing the term paper about a successful company which they must write for one of their courses.

Rosa: We should do our paper on Hotshot Inc. It's a great company.

Katy: Why do you think Hotshot is so great?

Rosa: Its founder is fabulously wealthy. He's worth billions! And it's all from this one company.

Box 4.2: Competitiveness as a value

"Life has become for us an endless succession of contests." Thus begins a critique by author Alfie Kohn of the value our society places on competitiveness.[1] Throughout our school years, he notes, we are trained to compete, to think of our classmates as standing in the way of our own success. The entire economic system is based on competition: "It is not enough that we struggle against our colleagues at work to be more productive; we also must compete for the title of Friendliest Employee."[2] Even when we socialize with people from other departments of the organization or other companies, this often takes the form of competitive games, like softball or golf.

The examples of competitiveness in the world of business are countless. Margaret Wente, a journalist with *The Globe and Mail* newspaper, notes that "the prevailing metaphors of business are borrowed from the battlefield. Your competition is the enemy, and your job is to grind them to dust. Takeovers are battles. Marketing is warfare."[3] The legendary Ray Kroc, the founder of McDonald's restaurant chain, once said: "What do you do when your competitor is drowning? Get a live hose and stick it in his throat!" Ricardo Petrella works in forecasting in the European Community Commission and decries what he calls the "gospel of competitiveness". One negative outcome he describes is accelerating obsolescence — firms must constantly develop new products, not because there is anything wrong with the old ones, but just because of the pressure to stay ahead of the competition.

Even when individuals or groups are not directly competing with one another, we seem to have an urge to compile rankings of who is best and who is not. Business magazines regularly publish lists of the top 100 firms, cutting across diverse industries. News magazines report on the best universities in the country. In 2004, a ranking of the wealthiest Canadians was made public. The late Ken Thompson, chairman of the publishing company Thompson Corp., with a net worth of over $22 billion, was in the number one position at the time. One is tempted to wonder: What exactly is the point of this ranking? In 2001, the federal government reported with concern that Canada's ranking in the ability to innovate had slipped to 16th place internationally. They set a goal to bring Canada to 5th place in the rankings by 2010. What will this mean to us? To others?

For many people, competitiveness is seen not just as the best way of doing things, but as "a fact of life" that is, the *only* way of doing things. Are there viable alternatives? One such alternative is co-operation — working with others, says Alfie Kohn. Or independence — comparing oneself not to others, but to an objective or self-set standard.

Notes
1. A. Kohn, *No Contest*, Revised edition (Boston: Houghton Mifflin, 1992), p. 2.
2. M. Lamey, "Downside Seen to Competitiveness", *Montreal Gazette*, June 8, 1992.
3. M. Wente, "Why I'll Never Be CEO", *The Globe and Mail*, October 25, 1992, D7.

Tom: Yes, she's right. I've read a lot about Mr. Hotshot and his company in the newspapers, and the company's share prices have been climbing steadily for years now.

Katy: Well I don't think that Hotshot's so wonderful. Sure, the top guys are making a lot of money, but the company is horribly exploitative. They treat their employees like dog turds, and they use strong-arm techniques to squeeze out their smaller competitors.

Rosa: But that's just business. You can't argue with success!

Rosa and Tom clearly value the *material success* of the entrepreneur and owners, whereas Katy places more importance on *corporate social responsibility* as a measure of what makes a firm successful. Katy does not deny the accuracy of the evidence provided about Mr. Hotshot's financial worth and the return on shareholders' investments. She just does not believe that profits are the most important aspect of what makes a great firm, so the financial information is dismissed as irrelevant. Rosa and Tom, with their focus on monetary worth, may also accept the characterization of Hotshot's business strategies, but they maintain that these practices are of little importance in evaluating the company. Each side could continue to add more evidence about financial success or about business strategies, but the additional evidence would not persuade the other side, since the disagreement about the underlying value assumptions remains. Can Katy persuade the other two that Hotshot's billions are not worthy of consideration? Can Rosa and Tom convince Katy that Hotshot's aggressive tactics are perfectly acceptable? It might be difficult in either case.

Values, as we have said, are often developed early in life and are quite resistant to change. It is not easy to make a profiteer out of someone who has been taught early in life that the love of money is the root of all evil. In the same way, it might take an extraordinary and jolting personal experience to create an iconoclast out of someone who has always believed in the value of obedience to authority. Not all values are so deep-seated, of course, but our value preferences form a significant part of our self-concept and are not relinquished lightly. In general, challenging value assumptions is a more difficult task than challenging descriptive assumptions. *The task of the critical thinker becomes one of demonstrating that the author's argument is rooted in a particular, idiosyncratic set of value assumptions. Since other people might have a different, but equally valid, set of values, the argument is therefore not universally acceptable.*

Effective writing

Critical thinking about underlying assumptions can help you to improve your own writing. A large quantity of evidence for your claims and ensuring that the evidence is of good quality are both necessary but not enough to be convincing. It is also important to make it clear that each piece of evidence is relevant. As you compose your text, articulate all your underlying assumptions and examine them with care. Keep asking yourself the following questions: Is this assumption *always* true? Are there circumstances in which the reality assumptions might not hold? Are there people whose value preferences might be different or in conflict with my own? Are all of the assumptions that underlie my argument logically consistent with one another? This self-questioning will allow you to understand the foundations of your own reasoning, and to spot any weaknesses in your argument before your readers do. One method that aids self-questioning about conflicting assumptions is the development of *invented dialogues*, described in **Box 4.3**.

Box 4.3: Invented dialogues

A fruitful way of exploring underlying assumptions is by constructing an **invented dialogue**. You start by imagining a discussion between two people who hold reality or value assumptions that conflict. This exercise is easier if you can think of people you actually know who have opposing views. Write a brief dialogue, about five or six exchanges between the two participants. Try to make their comments persuasive, lively, and natural. It often helps to read your dialogue out loud.

Here is an example of an invented dialogue between a Human Resource manager [HR] and a Vice-President, Operations [VP].

HR: Well, we've boiled it down to two potential candidates for the position. Both candidates have the relevant work experience and education. They both have impeccable track records with rave reviews from previous employers.

VP: Great! I'm looking forward to interviewing them myself.

HR: The first candidate is a woman in her mid-thirties who's been working...

VP: Hold on, a woman?!? You know we've never had a woman in this position before. She would have to supervise over 50 men. I sure hope your other candidate is a man.

HR: Come on, Eric. You know we can't discriminate against anyone based solely on gender.

VP: Who's talking about discrimination? We're talking about a person who will fit the shop-floor culture. I'm not against hiring a woman for a middle-management position, but we're talking here about the guys on the floor! They've never had to report to a woman before. Her life will be hell!

HR: Well, things will have to change around here, unless you prefer to have the Human Rights Commission knocking on our door. And then there's the Employment Equity bill which says....

VP: What the devil does the government know about our shop floor? We at headquarters understand about cultural diversity, and how it makes good business sense in a global environment. But this is a particular case. We simply can't hire a woman to handle those boys in the shop. It's a pretty rough environment down there.

(continued next page)

Box 4.3 (continued)

HR: Well, with your attitude, of course it will never work. If head office backs a woman, you'll send a clear message to everyone that we value people for their skills, not their sex or race.

VP: I can picture the guys' reaction already. I know it won't fly.

How would you characterize the conflicting assumptions of these speakers? Consider their reality and value assumptions about (a) the relative importance of education and experience; (b) compatibility with the company culture; (c) vigilance of government agencies; (d) gender roles; (e) impact of top management attitudes on workers; and so on.

Inventing dialogues of this sort can help you to clarify your own assumptions and train yourself to develop a richer understanding of alternative points of view.

Next, you must decide which of the assumptions you should include explicitly in the text and which can be left unstated. You may find that the majority of the assumptions are so obvious that they may remain implicit. But take care! What seems obvious to you may not be obvious to all your readers. In particular, if you can think of any circumstances in which your reality assumptions might not be true, it is best to describe these scenarios explicitly and limit your argument accordingly. Think about who your audience is likely to be. If they do not share your values, your carefully compiled evidence will be seen as irrelevant or wrong-headed. Think about the type of evidence that would be convincing for your expected readers. State your value preferences explicitly and argue for them so that your audience can at least appreciate your viewpoint. In the final chapter of this handbook, we will discuss *techniques of persuasion*, developing the notion of how a focus on your audience can help you to make your writing more convincing, even when your audience initially disagrees with you.

EXERCISES

Exercise 4.1

*What is the link between the claim and the evidence presented in the statements below? Describe the general principle that is the **underlying assumption** in each case.*

1. I don't want to work on a team with Philip. He talks constantly, and nobody can get a word in edgewise.

    Underlying assumption: People on a team should be allowed an equal opportunity to contribute ideas.

2. Gloria bought a new washing machine from Anvil Appliances last week, but it is malfunctioning. The people at Anvil should fix it or replace the machine with another.

3. Mrs. Carpenter ought to take better care of her husband. The shirt he is wearing today is not very clean, and his tie doesn't match at all.

4. Traffic jams in this city are becoming intolerable. Businesses should offer their employees flexible starting and quitting times.

5. Angela owns a thriving hardware store, but is currently short-staffed. Since her son is unemployed, Angela should offer him a job in the store.

6. Mr. Allard's rent on his vacation house is preposterously high — it's almost twice as much as he charged last year. He is taking advantage of the new golf course that has been built in the area.

7. That restaurant must serve good Chinese food. Look, almost everyone eating in there is Chinese.

Exercise 4.2: Underlying assumptions and values

Identify the claim and evidence in each paragraph. Discuss the underlying assumptions and values that are implicit here. In other words, what general principles link these claims with the evidence? Do you agree with these assumptions,; that is, do you believe that the evidence is relevant?

1. Commercial advertising should be allowed in university corridors and classrooms. In the past, senior university administrators have been calling for more university-business linkages; funds are sorely needed. We must expect that corporations will want to benefit from these arrangements by promoting their products. Second, everyone is bombarded with commercial advertisements on streets, in buses, and subways — everywhere. What difference does it make if people see the ads after they step into a university building? In any case, interviews show that most students and staff hardly notice the ads in our buildings.

2. Using the Internet causes people to become depressed and isolated. A research study conducted with a group of family members found that there were negative psychological effects after the family got access to the Internet. Although they socialized on the Internet using electronic mail, the participants were found to spend less time with their family and friends. Most home computers are set up in a den or bedroom, rather than a living room, where the computer user is likely to be around other people.

3. Workplace accidents in office settings are on the rise, while accident rates in industrial settings have been stable for years. A study conducted in 2008 found that accidents such as being crushed by elevator doors, collisions with other people or delivery carts, and falling down stairs had increased dramatically in the past five years in office settings. The increase in the practice of texting while walking from place to place is a major factor in the dramatic rise in workplace accidents in office settings. One recent business article suggested that texting while on the move was probably responsible for more than half of workplace accidents in office settings and that companies should ban texting at work in order to reduce accident rates.

4. A man should always have a workplace to go to. Even if you decide to retire, why would you want to stay at home? If you've gone to work every day, why would you just want to stop? After decades of work, you need to continue to be productive. What are you going to do with yourself? How long can you go bicycling, or sit on a beach, or watch golf on TV?

    How much volunteer work can you do? For most people, work of value is work that gets paid. The trick is not to have to do really onerous work. You should be able to turn down the volume without switching off completely. My father was a salesman, and at 85 years old, he was still going to an office, dealing with a few accounts. He didn't work very long — he was usually home by early afternoon — but he tried to go to work every day.

    Companies have a role, too. They have to realize that the population is aging — the boomers are hitting 65. Companies should offer employees continued employment with reduced or flexible hours. They could set up mentoring programs so that older workers can pass their expertise on to the next generation of employees. This will help companies to minimize the labour crunch that will come as the number of people available for work starts to decline. Better yet, the companies won't be losing the decades of experience that mature workers have developed, which is not written down anywhere. In fact, studies show that a majority of employers in the Americas, Europe, and Asia find that their older workers are more efficient and more loyal than their younger employees.

    And, finally, there has to be political action. Governments must reform pension rules to make having a more flexible retirement a serious possibility. Let's keep the golden years golden.

5. People continue to smoke against the advice of their doctors, therefore they should be put on the bottom of hospital waiting lists. There have been reports of British doctors who give lower priority to coronary operations for patients who persist in smoking. This would make good sense for the over-extended Canadian health system.

6. The U.S. Consumer Product Safety Association has concluded that adult beds are dangerous products as far as babies are concerned. A 1999 research study reviewed death certificates over a seven-year period and estimated that 64 infant deaths occur each year when babies sleep with their parents. The Association recommends that the practice of parents sleeping with their infants be outlawed. Many parents have reacted to this study with anger, noting that babies have slept with their parents since time immemorial and that the practice provides the attention, security, and nurturing that are essential for a happy, healthy family life.

Exercise 4.3: Advertising and underlying assumptions

A rich source of practice in uncovering and evaluating underlying assumptions is in the area of commercial advertising. Read the information in the box below, then do the exercise that follows.

> Some advertisements provide clear evidence for their claim that you should buy the manufacturer's product. They give you *relevant* information showing how use of the product will fulfill your needs, satisfy your desires, or solve your problems. Thus, for example, if you learn from an ad that a particular line of baked goods is made from whole grains with low sugar content, and you have been trying to make improvements in your diet and health, then the evidence in the ad is relevant to the claims that you should use these baked goods.
>
> But you will also see some ads that do not provide relevant evidence. Perhaps, for example, the baked-goods advertisement just shows a scene of a smiling, grandmotherly lady in a cosy, old-fashioned kitchen, bearing a tray of cookies. Maybe it portrays an elegant table set for afternoon tea — with polished silver tea service, fine linen napkins, and the manufacturer's product. Maybe we see a well-known athlete or actor enjoying the product. Advertisements like these rely on creating feelings of pleasure or admiration within us, and associating these feelings with the product. It is an emotional appeal, and the advertisers are counting on us *not* to analyze it rationally. When we do analyze it, however, we see that the underlying assumption is "because this ad makes you feel good, you should buy our product". No direct, relevant evidence is provided, so this type of advertisement does not justify a purchase. Unfortunately, these ads continue to be very successful for advertisers, since so few of us think critically about the underlying assumptions.

1. Watch television for a few hours, read a variety of popular magazines, or take a walk about town, paying special attention to the commercials, print ads, or billboards that you encounter.

2. Select three ads that provide relevant evidence about why you should purchase a product or service.

3. Select three ads that appear to be based on questionable underlying assumptions because they provide no relevant evidence.

4. In each case, describe the advertisement and explain what the advertiser is doing to increase the attractiveness of the product or service.

Exercise 4.4
Review Boxes 4.1 and 4.3. Write an invented dialogue between two university professors who have Theory X and Theory Y assumptions about their undergraduate students. Alternatively, invent a dialogue on a subject of your choice.

5

Causal Claims

Many of the claims authors make can be classified as causal claims. They argue that certain events or factors *(causes)* are responsible for bringing about other events or situations *(effects)*. Cause-and-effect relationships are an essential aspect of understanding the business environment. In fact, most of our attempts to make sense of the world around us — whenever we pose the question: *Why?* — lead to cause-and-effect explanations. "Why are sales of our firm's frozen foods falling?" "Why are there so few women CEOs in large companies?" "Why is there currently a boom in the home renovation industry?" "Why is Professor Merton so well liked by his students?" When we provide answers for these questions, we are identifying causes for observed outcomes. For example, we may determine that sales of frozen foods are falling because consumers are increasingly concerned about high salt content in their foods. In this cases, concern for salt content would be the cause; falling sales would be the effect.

Sometimes we know the "cause" and we are trying to predict the "effect". "What will happen if we decrease our printing budget by 15%?" "If we allow commercial advertising on the walls of public institutions like hospitals and schools, what reactions can we anticipate?" "What would be the result of an increase in the per litre tax on gasoline?" When governments make decisions about taxes on gasoline *(cause)*, there is much discussion about possible outcomes, such as increased use of public transit, decreased urban pollution, or increased prices of products that need to be transported *(effects)*.

Causal reasoning is natural — and useful

Trying to identify connections between causes and effects is basically human nature — as natural as breathing. Very young children start asking *Why?* as they take the first steps towards developing their understanding of the world. Much of our thinking is devoted to figuring out why things occurred and predicting what is likely to happen next. Without causal links between situations, nothing would make sense. Every event would be random and disconnected. Life would simply be a "buzzing, blooming confusion". The identification of causal relationships gives meaning to the world that surrounds us.

Cause-and-effect relationships are also the basis for decision making and reasoned action. For example, the belief that consumers' concerns about nutrition are changing might lead the marketing department of our firm to develop new products, such as low-sodium frozen foods. It is also likely to change the way these products are advertized.

Causal reasoning can be very difficult

Although we recognize the importance of establishing causal relationships, it is also true that doing so is very difficult. In the complex situations we encounter in the world of business, it is sometimes difficult to find reasonable and likely causes for certain outcomes. "Why is innovation lower in some countries than in others?" "Why is the presence of graffiti on the increase in our cities?" Causes can be elusive.

Even more frequently, the difficulty in determining cause-and-effect links arises from the fact that outcomes may have multiple causes. Let's say you notice that winter is over and you've managed to escape your usual winter cold. Well, you think, it must be because you've been drinking that special echinacea herbal tea your Aunt Minnie gave you, saying it is good for avoiding colds. You decide to call her and tell her it worked. But upon further thought, you realize there may have been other causes for your good health during the season. It was an unusually mild winter, with few dramatic swings of temperature. Also, since your new apartment is not far from downtown, you've been able to walk to school and your job instead of taking the bus, and so you have had less contact with other people. You've started exercising twice a week as well, and you recall reading somewhere that being in good physical shape helps to ward off colds. In short, there could have been many potential causes, so you are not sure any more that Aunt Minnie's herbal tea was really a cause of your cold-free winter. On their own, the other factors could well have caused your good health, quite independently of whether or not you drank the tea.

As critical thinkers, we must examine carefully the causal claims of authors. Are they describing genuine cause-effect relationships? Can we think of plausible *rival causal explanations* that would account for exactly the same events? If we can, then we do not really know whether it is the factor proposed by the author, the rival cause we came up with, or a combination of both causes that led to the observed effect. The author's claim becomes less convincing.

Let us now look at some examples of plausible rival causes. There are three types of rival causes that will concern us here: rival causes related to differences between groups; correlation between characteristics; and the *post hoc ergo propter hoc* fallacy. We will explain each of these in turn.

53

Differences between groups

An alumni survey produces evidence showing that graduates of Academy University are more successful on the job market than graduates of Ivory Tower University. The administrators at Academy claim that this success is caused by its superior programs — the up-to-date curriculum content, the talented teaching, and the advanced technological resources available at their institution. The top-notch facilities and programs cause its students to develop excellent, marketable skills, which impress company recruiters and lead to rapid and remunerative job offers. If you come to Academy University, their brochures claim, you'll do better than going to that other school.

Perhaps. But is the content of the academic programs the only difference between Academy and Ivory Tower graduates? It may turn out that Academy has more-rigorous admission requirements, so the students who *enter* their programs are smarter than the Ivory Tower students to start with. Even if Academy teachers had been dull as ditch water and used blackboard chalk instead of clickers, their smart students would still have excelled on the job market. Academy is claiming that their *programs* are the cause of their comparative success. Our rival cause is that their *selectivity in admissions* causes success. It is also possible that a combination of both factors is the true (multiple) cause. Another possibility is that Academy University is in an urban centre where many students have good part-time jobs, while Ivory Tower is in a rural setting and few students have part-time jobs of any consequence. It might be, then, that it is the *work experience* of the graduates that is causing the differences in success, and the academic programs are completely irrelevant.

In general, whenever an author says that an outcome is caused by a specific difference between groups, we must pause and think: *Are there any other differences between these groups that may be relevant?* If we can think of some other relevant factor that differs between the groups, we have a plausible rival cause.

Here's another example for you to think about. It has been noted that women who choose to have their babies at home have healthier babies than women whose babies are born in the hospital. One causal explanation that has been offered is that a hospital is an uncaring, unnatural environment and is no place for the natural function of bringing babies into the world. The heavy focus on medical technology in the hospital environment, and the stress this produces in pregnant women causes physical problems in newborn infants. People who believe this explanation often recommend that if a woman stays at home, and has her baby using the services of a midwife in familiar surroundings, there are psychological and physical benefits for both mother and child. Briefly put, the argument is that the hospital setting causes health problems in infants. Can you come up with plausible rival explanations of this relationship?

Correlation between characteristics

Here is an example of the type of writing often seen in the business press:

> It is important for all companies to have a strategic vision. What does your company stand for? What are your business values and mission? How do you see your future? Your firm's vision must be clearly communicated to employees at all levels of the organization. Business scholars have studied these "visionary" companies and found that they enjoy greater long-term success than other companies whose vision is less pervasive. The more careful you are to articulate a clear vision, the better the performance of your firm. Why? Because vision inspires employees and focuses their energies. Poor visioning leaves your resources scattered and your employees unmotivated. Start developing your vision now — don't get left behind!

The claim here is that a stronger company vision causes better performance. A weaker vision causes poorer performance. The authors have taken a *correlation* between these two factors and are claiming a *causal* link. Their explanation that a clearly communicated vision results in motivation and focus seems reasonable.

But is this the only explanation that will fit with the observations? Is it not possible that the link works in reverse? It may be that the better the performance of the firm, the more attention is paid to it in the media. Journalists visit the company, interview its managers, and write up their description of what it is that "makes the organization tick". The news reports are widely read, and the readers include the firm's own employees and managers, who end up with greater awareness and understanding of their company, its mission, and values. In this interpretation, it is the company's stellar performance that is causing the strong vision to develop. If this rival explanation turns out to be true, working on your company's vision is a dead-end strategy. Instead of vision causing performance, performance is actually causing vision. This is an example of *reverse causation*. In general, when two factors, A and B, are correlated, it may be that A is causing B, but it is also possible that B is causing A.

Yet another interpretation must be considered. Sometimes two factors may be strongly correlated, but there is no causal link at all between the two. It is well known, for instance, that when ice-cream consumption is high in a given year, the rate of heart attacks among the population is also very high. It would be absurd to suggest that eating ice cream brings on a heart attack within a year. It would be even more ridiculous to claim that when someone has a heart attack, this creates a craving for ice cream. Neither direct causation nor reverse causation is likely. The correlation is high because there is a *third factor* that is linked to both ice-cream consumption and heart attacks. This third factor, of course, is heat. The hotter the temperature, the more ice cream is eaten, and the hotter it gets, the greater the number of people who succumb to heart attacks. No matter how strong the correlation between two variables, we cannot automatically assume that there is a causal connection.

The ice-cream/heart-attack example is clear-cut, but in other cases it may be harder to see that causal links are not really there. Returning to the case of vision, it is possible that there is no causal relationship at all between the strength of strategic vision and firm performance. Perhaps there is a third factor linked to both vision and performance, say, the *use of information technology (IT)* in the company. Firms that embrace IT and other technological advances may be the better performers in their industries because they are the first to exploit the new technologies and cost efficiencies, or their employees may work longer hours because they can log in to the company site in order to work from home (that is, "use of IT" causes "performance"). As well, in technologically advanced companies, there may be much more communication among employees — using the company intranet, visiting the company website, and so on. The accessibility and sharing of information about the firm's strategies improves awareness and understanding of the vision among managers and employees (that is, "use of IT" causes "vision"). So there may be neither a direct causal link nor a reverse causal link between vision and performance, apart from the operation of this third factor, the use of IT.

Another third factor could be having an innovative and charismatic CEO. An innovative CEO makes decisions before the firm's competitors do, creating competitive advantage and better firm performance. An innovative CEO makes changes that catch the attention of employees, who talk about the new ideas throughout the company, creating a strong vision. Again, there may be no direct link between vision and performance.

In summary, a correlation between two factors might be explained by one of three causal links. There may be a direct causal relationship, a reverse causal relationship, or no relationship, except through the effect of a third factor. Whenever an author describes a correlation and proposes a causal explanation for this correlation, as critical thinkers we must ponder the likelihood of reverse causation as well as the third factor effect.

Now think about this case:

> Strong entrepreneurial ambition, that is, desire to start one's own business, has been found to be associated with lower interest in higher education. Several business thinkers have discussed this inverse correlation, arguing that people who have an entrepreneurial personality are "hands-on", creative, and risk-taking. Entrepreneurship is quite different from the world of higher learning, which tends to be structured, low-risk, and detached from the excitement of the real world of business. The stronger your entrepreneurial personality, the more likely you are to shun university, preferring to start your own company as early as possible.

Can you come up with other possible causal explanations of this link?

The *post hoc ergo propter hoc* fallacy

An opinion piece in a community newspaper reads:

> Community policing came to our neighbourhood last summer. The police officers are now much more accessible than they were before; they ride around the streets on bicycles instead of patrol cars, and they often wear shorts and look much more friendly than they used to. The new police station is much smaller than the old one and looks more inviting — you can see plants in the windows and there is occasionally an open-house where the neighbours can go in and meet the police officers. This new strategy is very effective. I read in the newspaper recently that acts of vandalism and theft have decreased in the neighbourhood over the past 12 months. I know I feel much more comfortable when I am walking home from work this summer.

The claim is that the community policing strategy has caused the decrease in crime. The reasoning appears to be that the police now have much more of a presence in the neighbourhood than used to be the case. Presumably, this increased visibility has discouraged would-be criminals, and so rates of criminal activity have gone down. But is this the only plausible explanation? It may be that the past 12 months have seen a high frequency of inclement weather — perhaps is has been colder, rainier, or snowier than usual — and this has kept people at home and off the streets, both the potential criminals and the potential victims. In other words, unusual weather would have led to a drop in the crime rate, whether or not the policing strategy had changed. Here's another possibility:

> Economic conditions in the city have been brighter over the past year than they had been for quite some time. There have been announcements in the newspaper that the unemployment rate is decreasing. The house construction and renovation markets are enjoying a surge of activity. If more people are finding jobs and are thus better able to make ends meet, this alone could have caused a drop in the crime rate, quite independently of the police officers' bicycles and open-house sessions.

Post hoc ergo propter hoc is a Latin phrase. Loosely translated it means: After this *(post hoc)* therefore *(ergo)* because of this *(propter hoc)*. *After* the new policing strategy was introduced, the crime rate decreased; *therefore*, we assume that the decrease in crime must have occurred *because of* the strategy. This is a fallacy, an error in our reasoning. Just because an event was followed by another event does not necessarily mean that the first event caused the second.

Superstitious behaviour often has its root in the *post hoc ergo propter* hoc fallacy. Some years ago, a student of mine came to an in-class test with a large key ring in the shape of a rubber animal, which he put on his desk. He had got the key ring from his girlfriend the previous term and happened to have it during a test he took. He did very well on the test, much better than he thought he would. Now the animal has become his test-taking mascot — always at his side to give him good luck. Having the animal and doing well on exams were associated, so he claims that the former caused the latter. I am certain that to a great extent, he was joking about this superstition, but it continues to affect his behaviour. Similarly, colleagues of mine have lucky ties, lucky pens, even a lucky restaurant in which to have lunch before a big presentation. All of these are claimed, tongue-in-cheek, to cause success at work. All started with events that were given a *post hoc ergo propter hoc* causal explanation.

A friend of mine was called Rita throughout her childhood and adolescence. When she started working and moved out on her own, she changed her name to Catherine. "Rita is an unlucky name," she maintains. "My life was miserable until I changed my name, so I don't want anybody calling me Rita again, and bringing problems into my life." If we apply our critical thinking skills to my friend's causal reasoning, can we come up with plausible alternatives as to what, apart from her new name, may be causing her presently happy life?

Can we ever be sure?

We have shown that there are often multiple causes for an outcome. Whenever an author makes a causal claim, it is generally not difficult for the astute reader to come up with a rival cause that provides an equally good explanation for the outcome. It may be that the author's proposed cause is indeed the correct explanation. Any one of the plausible rival causes that occur to the critical reader may be the true interpretation.

What is more, there may be *multiple causes*, that is, the correct explanation may involve more than one of these causal factors.

How, then, can we ever be sure about causal relationships? Can we ever rule out alternative causes and be confident that it is indeed one particular cause that leads to a given effect? Often, it is important that we be sure of what is causing what. What would be the point of long hours spent working on our company's vision statement if it is not the true cause of business success? Why invest in all the changes necessary for community policing if we are not sure that our investments will really pay off in a low crime rate? In the applied, practical world of business, we have to be confident about causal relationships if we are to avoid wasting money and human effort.

Experimental research

Testing causal claims is the raison-d'être of *experimental designs in business research*. The primary aim of an *experiment* is to rule out rival causal explanations. Experimental research designs increase our confidence in causal explanations. Here is an example of the simple experiment in business. Let's say that we want to determine the best schedule of rest breaks for call centre agents. Do they work most productively if they are given one hour for lunch, a 15-minute break in the morning, and a 15-minute break in the afternoon? Would it be better to allow agents to vary the length and timing of the breaks however they please, as long as the total is 90 minutes? We call these two scenarios the 15-60-15 schedule and the 90-variable schedule. The next step is to separate the agents into two groups, each of which works to one of the two schedules. After a few work days, we compare the productivity of the two groups and find that the productivity of the 90-variable schedule agents is higher than that of the 15–60–15 agents. We conclude that having flexibility in rest breaks causes higher productivity.

You can see that it would be important to ensure that there are no differences between the two groups *other than* the different schedules. If, for example, all the native English-speaking agents were put in one group and all the non-native speakers in the other, we would not know whether the productivity difference was due to language, schedule, or to both factors. Language would be a plausible alternative causal explanation. If one group had brand new equipment and the other group had older equipment, or if one group worked in a noisier environment than the other, differences in equipment or noise levels would be plausible alternative explanations.

Researchers use a technique called *random assignment* to ensure that the characteristics of the people in different experimental groups are identical. With random assignment, every call centre agent, whatever his/her language, gender, skill level, job tenure, etc, has an equal chance of being in either group. Researchers would also control variables such as noise levels, pay rates, etc., keeping them as similar as possible across groups so that they can rule out alternative causal explanations. Random assignment and control of extraneous variables help researchers to establish causal relationships with confidence. **Box 5.1** presents another example of an experiment in business.

Box 5.1: Charismatic leadership and task performance

What is the best kind of boss to have? One who inspires and excites you, one who helps you understand the details of the tasks to be done, or one who is friendly and concerned about your personal welfare? Business researchers label these three types of bosses as *charismatic* leaders, *structuring* leaders, and *considerate* leaders, respectively. Which of these three different leadership styles is best at motivating subordinates to work hard and effectively? Researchers Jane Howell, a professor at the University of Western Ontario, and Peter Frost, a professor at the University of British Columbia, conducted an **experiment** to examine this causal relationship between *leadership style* and *task performance*.[1]

(continued next page)

Box 5.1 (continued)

The research participants were 144 undergraduate business students at the University of British Columbia who were each asked to play the role of a general manager dealing with a pile of items in his or her in-basket. The in-basket contained letters, reports, and memos, and the participants had to exercise their managerial judgment about how to handle each item — making decisions, delegating tasks, requesting further information, and so on.

The task was presented to each student by a leader who used one of the three leadership styles. Although the participants did not realize it, the leader was actually an actor who had been carefully trained by the researchers to direct the work of the students using the three styles. As a *charismatic leader*, she presented an exciting goal, explaining how the task could foster links between the university and downtown businesses and would have a long-term effect on the future commerce programs at UBC. Her tone was engaging, her body language was dynamic, and she expressed confidence that the participant would perform very well at the task. As a *considerate leader*, she was friendly and approachable, showing concern for the comfort and satisfaction of the participant. Her tone was warm; she leaned towards the participant, smiling and keeping eye contact. As a *structuring leader*, she went through the directions point by point, explaining in detail how the task should be done and emphasized the standards of work performance. Her facial expressions and body language were neutral and business-like.

The participants were *randomly assigned* to one of the three experimental conditions. Apart from these differences in leadership style, however, they all worked in the same workroom, had the same in-basket exercise, and were given the same length of time to work on the task. The leader always followed the same scripts and wore identical clothes — a dark, conservative business suit. By *controlling* these extraneous variables, the researchers were ensuring that the only difference between the three groups of participants was the leadership style they encountered. They can have confidence, therefore, that the level of performance achieved by the students can be attributed to the type of leadership style and nothing else.

So how did it turn out? You may be interested to know that the researchers found that charismatic leadership caused the best task performance. Participants who had the charismatic leader had the highest quality of work and suggested the most courses of action in the in-basket task. The other two styles caused similar, lower levels of performance. The researchers concluded that training leaders to be charismatic is not only possible, but desirable. The study needs to be repeated in a "real-life" work place, but on the basis of this experiment, it would appear that the boss's charisma causes high task performance in subordinates.

Note
1. This research study was published in J. Howell and P. Frost, "A Laboratory Study of Charismatic leadership", *Organizational Behaviour and Human Decision Processes*, 43 (1989), 243–69.

This is just a very brief introduction to experimental research. Close study of how to conduct valid experiments is beyond the purview of this handbook, but it is important to note that experimental research in business has become an essential tool in improving our understanding of business practice. In **Box 5.2**, you will find a description of a classic set of experiments in organizational research.

Formal experimentation can be costly and is not a tool that can be applied to every question. Intelligent, critical thinking, however, can be. As readers and managers, it is always important to be able to discern when an author has a strong, well-supported causal claim, and when the causal claims are contestable and open to many interpretations. In the latter case,

---

Box 5.2: The Hawthorne experiments

The Hawthorne experiments were a series of large-scale experimental studies that formed an early milestone in the understanding of behaviour in organizations. Between 1924 and 1933, a group of investigators from the Harvard Business School conducted research studies at the Hawthorne plant of the Western Electric Company. The research was funded in part by manufacturers of electricity, who wanted to show that higher levels of electrical lighting would cause improvements in industrial efficiency.

One of the studies employed two groups of workers whose average skill and productivity was the same. The first group worked under a constant illumination of 11 foot-candles. (A foot-candle is equal to the amount of light thrown by one candle on a square foot of a surface which is one foot away.) The second group, the test group, were asked to work under progressively lower levels of light, going down to less than two foot-candles. The experimenters expected that the productivity of the test-group workers would decline as illumination got poorer. Instead, production increased in *both* groups. This increase in productivity was also found when the researchers changed other working conditions, such as the length and frequency of rest periods and the length of the work day. When improvements in working conditions were taken away after several months, production continued to rise.

It appeared that whether lighting, work schedules, and other working conditions were improved or made poorer, the productivity of the workers increased. In other words, any manipulation of working conditions, either for better or worse, improved productivity. The researchers concluded that variations in working conditions could *not* therefore be the *cause* of improved production. The cause seemed to lie in the fact that the workers who participated in the research were given *special attention* by the researchers and the plant managers. Getting special attention had been a much more powerful impetus to perform than any of the experimental conditions. This phenomenon has since been observed in innumerable experiments and has become known as the "Hawthorne effect".

Note: For more about the Hawthorne experiments, see F. Roethlisberger, and W. Dickson, *Management and the Worker* (Boston: Harvard University Press, 1966 [c. 1939]).

when we recognize the existence of alternative causal explanations, we must use our logic to assess the *likelihood* of each possible cause. The most likely cause (or causes) will shape our overall evaluation of the author's claims and the seriousness with which we will take her argument.

EXERCISES

Exercise 5.1: Causal thinking

Think about the following scenario:

> You arrive at the university library one Tuesday afternoon at 3 p.m. and find that the main doors are locked. What may be possible causes of this odd situation? Perhaps there was a gas leak or an electrical problem in the building, and the library was closed down temporarily. Maybe it is a public holiday you'd forgotten about, and the whole university is closed. There may be a problem with the doors, and if you look carefully, you'll see a sign telling you about an alternate entrance. Perhaps you're pushing instead of pulling, and the doors are not locked at all.

For most situations, there are a variety of causes that might explain a given effect. When an author proposes a particular causal relationship, the critical thinker must explore the plausibility of the causal link proposed, and decide whether there are other causes that are equally plausible or more likely.

Part I: In the following exercise, use your creative powers to suggest several possible causes for the given effects.

1. You've overslept three times in the past week.

2. Co-workers at your part-time job have suddenly stopped being friendly.

3. It takes you an hour to finish an exam that is scheduled to last for three hours.

4. Cars on a stretch of highway you drive every day seem to be going abnormally slowly.

5. Although overall industry sales are down, your product is exceeding projected sales figures.

6. Absenteeism in your department is higher in April than it was in March.

7. You didn't get the promotion you feel you deserved.

8. Every time you read your marketing textbook, you start to feel sleepy.

9. One of your less-talented subordinates is invited to lunch by your boss.

Part II: *In each case, what sort of evidence would you need in order to see which of your causal explanations is most probable? Where would you find this evidence?*

Exercise 5.2: Causal claims
In each of the passages below, identify the causal claim and the causal explanation offered. Can you think of a rival causal explanation? In other words, are there other plausible explanations for the relationship observed by the author? Draw on your understanding of differences between groups, association of characteristics, and the post hoc *fallacy to develop these rival explanations. Which of the explanations (including the author's) do you think is most likely?*

1. Workplace aggression is on the rise. Over 40% of employees in the United States report being the victim of psychological aggression at work — being shouted at, insulted, or threatened. About 6% were the victims of physical aggression, actually kicked, hit, or assaulted with a weapon. The aggressors were other employees, supervisors, and most frequently, members of the public. This increase in aggressive acts is the result of the stressful times in which we now live. The uncertain economy, with its attendant decreases in standard of living and fears of job loss, are causing customers to lash out at service employees, and employees to lash out at one another.

2. Over-achievers in the 1980s prided themselves on getting little sleep. In addition to long hours at the workplace, technological devices such as laptop computers, electronic mail, voice mail and the Internet make it possible to work into the wee hours of the night. Sleeping less meant they could work more and, thus, be more successful. By 2000, however, sleep had become a new status symbol for successful executives. Jeff Bezos of Amazon.com, Marc Andreesen of Netscape Communications Corp., and Michael Bonsignore of Honeywell were just a few of the extremely successful top-management executives who reported that getting eight hours of sleep each night left them refreshed, alert, and creative. This increased mental acuity played a major role in their success as executives. Today, insufficient sleep is more characteristic of less-successful managers lower down the totem pole.

3. Progressive firms have "family friendly" policies, such as provisions for extended parental leave, the possibility of job-sharing, flexible hours, telecommuting, or on-site daycare. This is more than just philanthropy — it makes good business sense. Employees in these firms can focus on getting their work done, knowing that child care is well managed and that if a problem does arise, they will be able to get the time to deal with it effectively. Working for a firm that is not

family friendly is considerably more stressful. In consequence, profitability is higher in a family-friendly firm.

4. My teammate, Noel, has said: "Whenever I dream about my old high school, the project on which I am currently working runs into problems. I experienced a lot of anxiety during high school, and these dreams come like a sort of warning. Twice, recently I had dreams about high school and, look, our mark for this team project is only a C minus. It's not just superstition — this is how it turns out every time."

5. The role of the board of directors of a firm is to act in the shareholders' best interests, actively guiding the long-term management of the firm. In practice, board members may end up passively "rubber-stamping" top-management decisions. Some scholars advocate that board members should be required to have significant stock ownership in the firm in order to ensure that they take an active interest. Research has found that the larger the stock holdings of a firm's board members, the more profitable the firm and the higher the share prices. This is because the share-holding board members have substantial stakes in the company's success. They are therefore more likely to look closely at the actions of management and make sure that managerial decisions are sound.

6. Daylight savings time is hazardous. The day after we move the clocks forward in the spring, car accidents increase by 7%. This dramatic change is due to the loss of one hour's sleep. In the fall, the day after we turn the clocks back and gain an hour's sleep, accidents decrease by 7%.

7. Many companies have recruitment programs that encourage current employees to refer outside applicants for job openings. In one such program at a large U.S. bank, a review of over 5,500 job applications found that 35% of the people who were referred by employees were hired, while only 3% of the other applicants got jobs. The greater success of referrals comes because their friends provide inside information about when to present one's resumé, the exact skills that are required for the job, and so on. Outsiders have little hope when competing against people with this privileged information from their personal connections. It really is who you know that counts in landing a job.

6

Techniques of
Persuasion

W hat makes an argument persuasive? How do authors convince readers to agree with their point of view? A variety of factors, several of which we have encountered in the earlier chapters, affect the persuasiveness of a text. Certainly the *quality of the evidence* presented for the claims is one such factor; we are persuaded when the evidence is accurate, precise, sufficient, representative, authoritative, and clear. But just as it is essential to evaluate the evidence that is *presented,* it is equally important to think about the evidence that is *omitted.* Think, for example, of the possible reaction of an author who encounters a piece of evidence that contradicts his claim. In composing his text, he decides to omit several bits of data that are inconsistent with the conclusion that he wants to draw. As critical thinkers, we must ask ourselves: What evidence is left out because it is incompatible with the argument?

The *soundness of the causal argument* also makes a text persuasive. Yet it often happens that evidence presented may be compatible with more than one causal interpretation. When alternative causal explanations exist, this undermines confidence in the author's conclusion. For example, having found evidence of a strong relationship between A and B, the author might believe strongly that A caused B, but knows that another interpretation is that B caused A, a reverse causal explanation. How do writers deal most effectively with this problem of *rival explanations*?

Finally, we have seen that the extent to which readers *agree with the underlying assumptions* of a writer plays an important role in their decision to accept or challenge the author's claims. *Conflicts in value preferences or reality assumptions* are common. How can an author be persuasive when her audience may not share her underlying beliefs or values?

The foregoing issues are related to the basic structure of an argument — claims, evidence, and assumptions. A further aspect to be considered is the language and writing style used in the text. How does an author present her case most effectively, bringing her readers to appreciate fully the significance of her evidence? Do her words capture our attention and imagination, bringing her claims into clear (and persuasive) focus? In this chapter, we shall also introduce *rhetoric,* which is the use of language to convince.

A "how-to" approach

The approach taken in this chapter is to describe *how to* build a persuasive argument; we shall then use this information to understand why certain authors are convincing, while others are not. We answer the questions posed above, deciding how to deal with contradictory evidence, alternative causal explanations, and value conflicts, in a way that will be most persuasive to an audience. We take a brief look at effective use of words and other rhetorical devices that help us to present our claims most convincingly. Again, it must be stressed that we are *not* recommending that words be used as a smokescreen to conceal weak reasoning. As critical thinkers, we must always analyze the structure of the argument (claim, evidence, and assumptions), however well or poorly the argument is worded. What we *are* advocating is clear and vivid writing that puts the reader in the author's shoes and allows him to live the experiences of the author or her sources.

The following sections discuss general strategies for building a persuasive argument. First, we look at how to deal with objections to the structure of your argument. Next, we focus on how to use language persuasively.

A theme that will come up repeatedly is the important requirement that you *think about your audience*. How much do your readers already know about the issue under discussion? How familiar might they be with the evidence you are about to present? Have they already formed their own ideas about the issue, and are they likely to agree or disagree with your claim? What might be the values that underlie their beliefs? Granted, you rarely will know all these details about the beliefs and values of everyone who is likely to read your work. Further, you may have to write for a very diverse audience, making it more complicated to tailor your argument to a particular group. As we shall see, however, the more you think about your potential readers, the stronger the argument you can build. Forewarned is forearmed.

Anticipate and counter readers' objections

The first step in writing persuasively is a brainstorming, troubleshooting process in which you should put yourself in the shoes of your audience and perform "destructive testing" on your ideas. What objections could possibly be made to your argument? If your readers are fully engaged critical thinkers, they will continually be consulting their own knowledge and beliefs, and will undoubtedly raise questions as they watch your reasoning develop. Recall that most interesting claims in the study of business tend to be *contestable* claims, so it is small wonder that they will be contested! If readers' objections are unaddressed in your writing, your claim will be dismissed out of hand. It follows that if you want to be persuasive, your job is to answer these expected questions as they arise. To do this, you have to present the question or objection explicitly, then provide a convincing answer or rebuttal in your text. By mentioning and refuting objections, you will show your readers that you have considered the issue fully. If you *don't* address their concerns, they will simply think that it was your ignorance or naivete that led you to such a wrong-headed conclusion!

Some common types of objections that you can anticipate occur when (i) readers are aware of negative evidence that refutes your claim; (ii) readers can come up with alternative causal explanations that are consistent with your evidence; and (iii) readers disagree with your value preferences or reality assumptions.

Negative evidence

The world is a complex and contradictory place, and it is rare that every piece of evidence that bears on an issue will lead irrevocably to a clear and unassailable conclusion. In fact, when they are doing research to support a claim, writers often have the experience of finding data and descriptions of events that run counter to the claim. So it should not be surprising that some readers are bound to think of contrary evidence that would undermine your argument. If you are aware of negative evidence, the sensible response is to present such evidence in order to show that you have given it due consideration. Thus, you will show that, properly interpreted, it is not negative, that it actually is not reliable, or that its importance is overstated. Consider how you might deal with very salient — and widely believed — evidence that contradicts your thesis about crime:

> In summary, the crime rate is definitely on the decrease. Statistics from major cities across North America show this. However, when we read newspapers, watch television, or go to the movies, it would appear that crime and violence are rampant. These reports cannot be disregarded. Crime news, both on TV and in newspapers, is much more explicit than it used to be; things that used to be passed over are now shown and described in full graphic detail. Movies that horrified people 20 years ago are just commonplace now. "Gangsta rap" is chic. Crime has become entertainment. But depictions of violence must not be mistaken for the phenomenon itself. Although it *seems* as though we are inundated with crime, this is quite misleading. The crime rate is indeed falling.

Or, perhaps, your claim is that successful entrepreneurs are very independent, but you know that there is a lot of focus on business networks as sources of advice for the entrepreneur. Again, you would mention the negative evidence and then show why it is misleading:

> Many research surveys conclude that successful entrepreneurs have large networks of business colleagues and advisers. That, at least, is what the entrepreneurs say on paper-and-pencil questionnaires. But when we use a less-superficial research technique, the in-depth interview, entrepreneurs go on to admit that they rarely use these networks for advice about business problems, and when they do, they find the advice they get is not particularly helpful. The

networks may be there, but when it comes to advice about running the business, successful entrepreneurs make their own decisions and are fiercely independent.

Rival causes

If the claim you are proposing is a causal claim, it is likely that there are rival causal explanations of your evidence. Recall that plausible rival causes may be located in differences among groups, reverse causation, the effect of a third variable, or the *post hoc* fallacy (see Chapter 5). Certainly, if you can think of a possible rival cause, it makes no sense to just keep quiet about the problem and hope that readers will not see the hole in your argument. It is guaranteed that some careful reader will catch the problem, especially if he or she disagrees with your claim. So, as part of the brainstorming process, you must discipline yourself to find and propose alternative causes, then rebut them, showing the reader why they are unlikely to be the real explanation. For example:

> All the firms we studied devoted a great deal of time and resources in managing relationships with their clientele. This relationship marketing was pivotal in ensuring their profitability. We considered the possibility that only profitable firms could afford to spend time focusing on relationship marketing. Could success have preceded their use of this marketing approach? A careful review of the history of each firm showed that the focus on client relationships generally came before they were successful. From the very beginning, the entrepreneurs emphasized the importance of getting to know the needs and personalities of their clients. It was not success, then, that caused this strategic approach. Rather, the strategy led to the ultimate success of the enterprise.

As another example, consider how the systematic consideration and rejection of other explanations, anticipates the reader's questions about the causes of good course evaluations:

> The students who were in small classes gave the course much higher ratings than the students in the large classes. Note that the time of day the course was held, the proportion of full-time and part-time students, and the average GPA of the students were all uncorrelated with the ratings. Moreover, most of the instructors taught both large and small sections, so it was not the skill of the instructors that made the difference. We can conclude, therefore, that it was the small class size that caused students to be more enthusiastic about their courses.

Debatable assumptions

In Chapter 5, we discussed how critical thinkers can challenge underlying reality assumptions and values: first, they make the author's assumptions explicit, then they present counter-arguments to show that the assumptions are incorrect. To write persuasively, then, you must anticipate these challenges to your assumptions. If you know that there are reality assumptions that your audience might feel are debatable or wrong, you must provide explicit data to back up your assumptions. Here is an example:

> The series of workshops on stress relief for executives, organized by the Employee Assistance Program, has been a great success. A survey conducted by the HR department showed that workshop participants were enthusiastic about the sessions and reported that the stress–reduction techniques had a substantial positive impact on their performance on the job. Management should move quickly to make the program available to all employees. *Of course, this assumes that lower-level employees could benefit from stress reduction just as much as those at the executive level can. And there is no question that this assumption is warranted.* Studies show that first–line supervisors, sales representatives, secretaries — people in a variety of jobs — experience stress in this complex world of rapid change and uncertainty.

Since stress, in the popular imagination, is often associated with high-powered, high-responsibility executive jobs, you have to anticipate that this reality assumption will lead some readers to disagree with your claim. So you deal with it explicitly, refuting the erroneous assumption with data.

When your readers' values differ from your own, again, your job is to show them that your values are worth serious consideration. Some values may be just based on unthinking tradition and a feeling that "... well, doesn't everybody think the way I do?" In this case, people have not actively questioned some of their values. If your writing poses a strong and logical challenge to their value assumptions, they may discover that they are not all that strongly committed to certain values. In cases like this, you have a chance of persuading them to reflect on, and perhaps accept, your viewpoint. Let's say, for example, that a reader believes an individual's right to privacy is important, but has not really thought carefully about what that might mean in a business context. You will need to anticipate this value conflict, and your counter-argument will show the reader that the case for individual privacy is not clear-cut. Perhaps seeing your rationale might actually sway the reader to agree with your position.

> Pzasz Executive Search has thorough and reliable head–hunting procedures. They are the consultants of choice for recruiting a senior administrator for our university. Their investigators research the accuracy of all resumé items, follow up on all references, and check with a variety of past co–workers about the candidate's credentials, character, and integrity. They have even been known to question neighbours about the good citizenship of prospective administrators. Now, some may feel that this close investigation invades the privacy of the individual. But let us balance the value of individual privacy against our responsibility to our institution. We need ethical leadership. Good moral character is demanded of teachers, police chiefs, and heads of state. So, too, in university administrators. This person will represent our institution to the

world, and must serve as a role model for hundreds of academics and tens of thousands of students. Let us ensure that our choice is a good one.

Limit your claims when you have no rebuttal

What of the objections that you can anticipate, but for which you cannot find a plausible rebuttal? It happens, even to the most practised researchers and writers. You must concede points that you cannot refute. This concession may take various forms.

1. Limits to your generalizations: *All our evidence is drawn from large, high-tech corporations. Further research is necessary before we can confidently extend the claim to smaller firms, or those in other, more mature, industries.*

2. An assessment that the level of probability of your claim is less than 100%: *Although the evidence for my conclusion is mixed, it still is very probable that when firms embrace environmental sustainability goals, profitability increases; the few contradictory cases are far outweighed by the evidence that is consistent with my claim.*

3. A refinement or re-defining of your terms: *I've been arguing that entrepreneurs born outside of Canada are more dedicated to growing their firms and going global than entrepreneurs who are native Canadians. Admittedly, Guy Laliberté of the Cirque du Soleil and Alain Bouchard of the Couche-Tard convenience-store chain are counter-examples. However, both these businessmen are from Quebec and it can be argued that Quebec is different from the rest of Canada. The key success factor, then, may be one's status as an outsider — a businessperson who is outside the Canadian business establishment.* (This paraphrases an argument made by Andrea Mandel-Campbell in her 2007 book, *Why Mexicans Don't Drink Molson.*)

It may seem to you that making these concessions and describing limitations to the truth of your claims weakens your argument. Actually, it does just the opposite. It is paradoxical, but true, that *acknowledging limitations makes your writing more persuasive*. By considering the full complexity and nuance of the claim, you show yourself to be thoughtful and judicious. Readers can see that you have weighed pros and cons and used your critical powers of judgment to reach a conclusion. If an author just presents a "bare-bones" claim-and-evidence text, her argument often seems naive, if not downright simple-minded.

Rhetoric

In this section, we consider how the use of language affects the credibility and persuasiveness of your argument. Language is the primary tool to communicate thinking. One of the attributes that sets human beings apart from other animals is our ability to convey complex, abstract, or personal experiences to other human beings through speech, reading, and writing. Some writers know how to use language well; others are sloppy, imprecise, and therefore unconvincing. Some people are good at conveying emotions with their words — they create in their readers and listeners feelings of anger, pride, indignation, fear, etc. The art of using language to persuade is known as *rhetoric*. We study rhetoric to understand the techniques used by authors and speakers to convince an audience of the rightness of their views. **Box 6.1** provides an analysis of the rhetoric commonly used by textbook writers.

Box 6.1: The rhetoric of textbooks

The world of business organizations is an unpredictable place. When we read the business news, work as employees in organizations, observe managers at work (see **Box 2.1**), or make decisions about our stock market investments, our impression of the business environment is characterized by ambiguity and uncertainty. Firms can be so fragile — here today and gone tomorrow. Managers may be "downsized" without warning. Technological advances, cultural diversity, and globalization create constant change, unpredictability, even chaos in the world of business.

Yet, how are business organizations portrayed in introductory business textbooks? Stephen Fineman and Yiannis Gabriel have pointed to an interesting gap between the unpredictability of today's organizations and the way in which these organizations are portrayed in introductory textbooks. The researchers studied textbooks on organizational behaviour, but their conclusions are probably applicable to textbooks in other disciplines of business. The standard textbook, Fineman and Gabriel argue, does not reflect our current understanding of business but portrays organizations as structured, solid, and stable. Their contention is that the *rhetoric of the textbook* makes this portrayal inevitable. The rhetorical devices commonly used in textbooks — definitions, case studies, and lists — all make it appear that the information presented is factual, not contestable.

Definitions are usually highlighted or placed in boxes or margins for emphasis. Definitions convey the idea of science, precision, and rigour. They represent a conveniently sized piece of information that can be memorized and reproduced in examinations and reports. By their very nature, definitions encourage students to accept the information presented as indisputable facts.

Case studies are often used in textbooks to illustrate concepts. It might seem that case studies can demonstrate the chaos and unpredictability of "real life". Typically, they do not. The "characters, plots, and narrative are condensed, reduced to a minimalist state ... [which serves to] reinforce the image of organizations as orderly and impersonal" (pp. 382–83).

(continued next page)

Box 6.1 (continued)

Lists aid memorization but eliminate argument. Authors rarely present their arguments for the inclusion or exclusion of elements on the list. Too often, learning comes to mean associating a list of authors' names with theories, and each theorist with a list of key terms.

In general, then, the definitions, case studies, and lists that are characteristic of textbooks leave the reader with the impression that the facts are clear. The effect of these devices is practically to eliminate critical thought, argument, and debate.

Buying an introductory textbook is a part of "rite of passage" into a discipline that is new to the student. Since it is establishing the discipline in the student's mind, the emphasis is on what is known, on the power of the discipline. Everything seems clear-cut and well understood. "The textbook is a ticket to a club, a fount of knowledge and a guarantee of safe passage" (p. 379). Issues that raise too many questions are necessarily excluded as inviting unwanted ambiguities. As a result, the turbulence that characterizes the real world of organizations vanishes, and the reader is left with an inaccurate picture of organizational stability and orderliness.

Note: For Stephen Fineman and Yiannis Gabriel's complete argument, see "Paradigms of Organizations: An Exploration in Textbook Rhetorics", *Organization*, 1, 2 (1994): 375–99.

You may have heard people speak disparagingly of rhetoric, often when using the phrase, "empty rhetoric". In this construction, rhetoric means the use of language that is artificial, elaborate, and showy, with little real substance to support the arguments. Rhetoric in this sense usually involves a deliberate intent to mislead. There is a vast public relations industry whose major task is to ensure that the information that people get about the corporate world is presented in the best possible light (see **Box 6.2**). It is unfortunate that language can be used to manipulate readers and conceal insincerity, but it should be equally obvious that not all people who use words effectively are hypocrites. People also use language to convey sincerely held opinions, to inform, enlighten, and share their human experiences. The existence of spin doctors should not lead to a cynical rejection of rhetoric. Most students of rhetoric are people who want to convey their ideas as clearly and accurately as possible.

Here follows a brief overview of some of the rules of rhetoric.

Be complete

The first rule is that you must present your reasoning in full and clear detail, since much of the evidence you present will be new to the reader. The world of business is vast, and a multitude of issues and events are sub-

---

Box 6.2: Press releases and the business news

Where do newspaper reporters get information for their articles? A substantial portion of the business information we read in newspapers comes from **press releases** written by the firms themselves and transported, holus-bolus, into the news articles. **Press conferences** are often called when major firms are changing their leadership or introducing new products. As we might expect, the information presented to the news media in press releases and at press conferences is carefully worded by skilled public relations professionals to make the firm look efficient, progressive and successful. They are written to produce what PR specialists have termed "good ink". So to the extent that rushed and harried reporters rely on the information and even the wording of press releases (conveniently crafted for this purpose), it may be unwise to expect that articles reported in newspapers are unbiased facts. There's another factor that creates bias in business reporting. Too much bad press might lead companies to withdraw their advertisements, and corporate advertisements are an important source of revenue for newspapers. For most newspapers, advertisements typically bring in much more revenue than individual and subscription sales of the newspaper to readers. It is little wonder that the news is full of flattering stories and glowing reports about business.

---

sumed under the heading of business studies. Even experienced managers and business scholars cannot keep track of it all. It is important to present your writing with sufficient points to allow potential readers to make the connection to their own experience. Moreover, you will have spent a lot more time thinking about your particular argument than most of your readers. You have worked hard to collect evidence and to organize it into a coherent position. Use your evidence thoroughly — to its maximal potential. This does not mean a painstaking reconstruction of all your initial mistaken thoughts, your difficulties in finding reliable evidence, or all the blind alleys you ran into as you developed your ideas. But do give enough detail (within your space or time restrictions) to allow your audience to appreciate fully the import of your data and logic. Undeveloped ideas and an assumption that your audience will "fill in the blanks", are not persuasive.

Use an appropriate tone

When you write, you create a relationship between yourself and your audience. This relationship may be quite formal and distant, or it may have a more informal and personal quality. The quality of the writer/reader relationship that is inherent in your writing is known as *tone*. By thinking of your future readers, you can decide whether a formal, *scholarly* tone or a less formal, *narrative* tone would be more appropriate.

The scholarly tone is characterized by rational exposition of the structure of your argument. Logic is highly prized. The scholarly tone uses formal, technical language or abstract analysis, and makes frequent reference to the ideas of academic experts and researchers in the field. Academic journals and most textbooks are written in this way. Citations, footnotes, and reference lists are standard. In some areas of business, scholarly writing is very mathematical. Essentially, the scholarly tone is an *appeal to authority*.

The narrative tone is characterized by stories and anecdotes. Vividness is emphasized. The writer uses many descriptions and examples, sometimes including actual quotations from managers, customers, consultants, etc., where they are relevant to the argument. Striking personal experiences, first-hand observations, and dramatic case studies are frequent when writers use a narrative tone. Business newspapers and magazines, as well as popular business trade books, tend to use this tone (see **Box 6.3**). The narrative tone often entails an *appeal to emotion*.

Box 6.3: Marketing myopia and the power of rhetoric

Theodore Levitt, a professor of marketing, wrote an extremely popular article in a 1960 issue of the *Harvard Business Review*.[1] Levitt's major claim was that firms should think of themselves, not in terms of the particular product or service they offer, but in terms of the broad industry within which the product or service is located. Railways, for example, should define themselves as operating in the transportation industry; oil companies are in the energy business. This broader focus will ensure companies' continued growth, even in the face of technological change. Why? Because transportation will always be necessary, even if rail travel is eroded by growing use of cars, airplanes, and trucks. Since all particular products (and services) are bound to be obsolete eventually, a *product* orientation is therefore myopic. A *customer* orientation, on the other hand, offers more growth opportunity in an environment of technological change. Firms that focus heavily on production methods, and on product research and development, but ignore customers and markets are said to be suffering from **marketing myopia** and are destined for obsolescence.

Levitt's article was enormously influential. His ideas were put into practice by airlines, publishing houses, car companies, oil companies, shoe stores, and cosmetic firms, among others. In the first fifteen years after its publication, *Harvard Business Review* sold over a quarter of a million reprints of the article. The results of implementing these ideas have been mixed. Some firms benefited greatly from this heightened awareness of the market in which they operated, but some others ended up defining themselves so broadly that they lost focus and diversified into inappropriate areas. In the words of one of Levitt's critics, "Why should a few clever words on a piece of paper enable a railroad company to fly airplanes, or for that matter, run taxicabs?"[2]

(continued next page)

Box 6.3 (continued)

In a retrospective commentary, Levitt pondered the astounding impact of his article: "Why its appeal throughout the world of resolutely restrained scholars, implacably temperate managers and high government officials, all accustomed to balanced and thoughtful calculation? Is it that concrete examples, joined to illustrate a simple idea and presented with some attention to literacy, communicate better than massive analytical reasoning that reads as though it were translated from the German? Is it that provocative assertions are more memorable and persuasive than restrained and balanced explanations, no matter who the audience?"[3]

Levitt is suggesting that it was primarily the **rhetorical quality** of his article that accounted for its success, in particular, his use of a strong **narrative tone**. The article is full of vivid, colourful examples of Hollywood movie producers, the first supermarkets, oil companies, and car manufacturers. He makes dramatic over-statements of his case, suggesting, for example, that product-oriented engineers in R&D see customers as "unpredictable, varied, fickle, stupid, shortsighted, stubborn, and generally bothersome". He describes a Boston millionaire who declared that his entire estate should be invested solely and forever in streetcars because of his myopic belief that this product would always be in demand. He mentions John Rockefeller creating a market by sending free kerosene lamps to China. These and other examples combine to grab the readers' attention and make his article very convincing.

Notes
1. T. Levitt, "Marketing Myopia", *Harvard Business Review*, Sept./Oct. (1975). Reprint of 1960 article.
2. H. Mintzberg, *The Rise and Fall of Strategic Planning* (New York: Free Press, 1994), p. 280.
3. T. Levitt, *Marketing Imagination* (New York: Free Press, 1986), p. 14.

Determining your tone means thinking about your audience. Publishers usually know who their main audience is, and business authors choose their tone depending on where their work will be published. As a business student, you should probably aim for a middle ground in your writing. You will want to demonstrate to your teachers that you are becoming increasingly familiar with the work of scholars in your field of study. At the same time, business studies is an *applied* field, and it is equally important that you learn to write for an audience of business practitioners who might be suspicious of, or bored by, a strictly academic style. As will be argued in the next section, even the most analytical, matter-of-fact texts can profit from vividness and detail, if the author wants to be convincing.

Be vivid

By using vivid language, you bring your evidence to life, attracting attention to your points and making them memorable for your readers. In this section, we shall mention a few techniques that are commonly used to make writing more vivid, and therefore more persuasive. These brief pointers, however, are no substitute for a good guidebook on writing style. Countless style guides exist that are invaluable aids for the beginning, as well as the experienced writer. Find one you like and use it regularly.

As you read the following report from an employee newsletter, ask yourself whether vivid images of the event and its impact on the employees' morale spring to mind.

> The meeting was well attended and pretty interesting. The division manager said that profits were low last quarter, and people were not too happy, but a new supplier has made a good offer to provide raw material at a more reasonable cost, and there is a window of opportunity to bring in some high-tech equipment soon. This means that by next year things should be better in the division, especially if there is belt-tightening in other areas, so by the end of the meeting people felt pretty good about that.

Why is this piece not vivid? First, there are many **vague words**, words that are imprecise and do not stimulate readers' imaginations. "Interesting", "low", "reasonable", and "pretty good" are vague. In the paragraph, few **concrete details** are provided to make the incident memorable. Metaphorical phrases like "window of opportunity" and "belt-tightening", which may once have been vivid, have been so over-used in business writing that they are now listless **clichés**. Now we rewrite the text, replacing vague words more precise ones, providing concrete details of the setting of the meeting and the actual words of the participants, all of which are designed to bring the event to life for the readers. Fresher, more vigorous phrases take the place of the cliches.

> Practically the entire department attended the open meeting, which was originally scheduled to meet in the departmental training room. Because of the unprecedented numbers, the meeting had to be moved to the board room. The extraordinary interest was a result of last month's financial results: profits had plummeted from $460,000 a month to just over $135,000. What had gone wrong? Who was to blame? Anxiety levels were high.
>
> The fundamental problem according to Bert Sheldon, the manager, was skyrocketing raw material costs. Lupu Inc., the regular supplier, had changed its pricing policy with scarcely any notice. That, together with a tightening supply market, caused raw material costs to go up 22%, all but wiping out profit. He had remonstrated with Lupu at the highest level, but to no avail. So two decades of working with Lupu ended in a call for bids. A new arrangement now exists with Playfair & Long who, in exchange for an exclusive contract, will supply us at 5% less than the spot rate on the London Metal Exchange. Moreover, P & L can supply and install high tech sealant machines which, in the long run, should reduce operating costs by 2 to 3 percent. Initial financing costs are hurting, but with a sharp eye kept on other costs, strong performance is expected within a year.

> The meeting left employees with a clear signal that head office has the situation firmly in hand. The initial glum atmosphere was entirely dispelled, and optimism reigned.

Rewritten, the text is considerably longer, but much easier to visualize. The use of precise, vivid language convinces the reader of the importance of the meeting and conveys clearly the shift in morale among the employees. Again, it cannot be emphasized enough that almost all writers rely on dictionaries, thesauruses, and style guides to help them seek appropriate words and phrases, to ensure correct usage, and to rise above vagueness and cliche.

Effective reading

The intelligent use of rhetoric, then, goes hand-in-hand with the development of a sound, logical argument. Neither aspect is sufficient by itself. By analogy, when you have cooked a delicious meal, you want to be sure to serve it on a clean plate with an attractive table setting. It detracts greatly from good food if it is served on dirty dishes or in unappetizing surroundings. Everyone appreciates a skilful wordsmith, but if your argument is not sound and you try to cover up its deficiencies with emotional or authoritative language, then you are encouraging fallacious thinking. As a writer, you must make every effort to ensure that there is substance underlying your well-crafted prose.

You cannot assume, however, that all writers marry a sound argument with persuasive writing. It sometimes happens that an author's excellent command of rhetoric is accompanied by a weak argument structure. As a critical reader, your first task is to expose and criticize the bare bones of the argument — the claims, evidence, and assumptions, independently of the rhetorical devices that the author added for impact and readability.

And consider the other possibility. Occasionally, you will encounter a writer who has a poor command of language and style. Try not to be distracted; invaluable ideas may often be found in unappealing packages. Again, by focusing on claims, evidence, and assumptions, you may find that the awkward prose conceals a treasure trove of intellectually stimulating information.

EXERCISES

Exercise 6.1: Vague words

"A *middle-aged* acquaintance of mine recently decided to leave a *high-paying* job in a *large city* to take instead a *low-paying* job in a *small town*."

Part I: Replace each of the italicized words with a precise number that seems appropriate:

middle-aged	=		years old
high-paying	=	$ _____	as an annual salary
large city	=	_____	residents
low-paying	=	$ _____	as an annual salary
small town	=	_____	residents

Part II: Ask five other people to do this exercise. Try to find people of varying ages and backgrounds. Compare the answers you get.

Exercise 6.2: Removing rhetorical flourishes

Part I: Read the following passage and rewrite it using simple, factual prose. Eliminate emotional language, the colourful phrases, and the rhetorical devices that are intended to persuade the reader. Afterwards, compare the original to your rewrite. What is your reaction to the differences?

Productivity problems? What company is immune? When your personnel costs are high, even small improvements in your workers' efficiency can make a big difference to your beleaguered bottom line. Professor Kevin Warwick, a leading researcher in cybernetics at Reading University in England, may have the answer — in a tiny silicon chip.

Prof. Warwick's cutting-edge research made headline news in the summer of 1998 when the intrepid scientist arranged to have a silicon chip implanted in his own arm. He demonstrated that all his movements could then be monitored on a computer, via receptors which were located at various positions in the building where he worked. Subsequent tests on other volunteers have allowed him to perfect this technique of tracking the whereabouts of individuals as they wander about designated buildings.

As a measure of timekeeping and efficiency, the business potential of this scientific breakthrough is exciting. And at a cost of just a few dollars per employee, improved productivity is rarely to be had so cheaply. According to the *London Times*, Prof. Warwick has been approached by several firms who are eager to learn more about this new technology.

Part II: Rewrite the passage once more, this time from the point of view of someone who wants to persuade the reader that this is a dangerous innovation.

Part III: Read the following passage and rewrite it to increase its vividness. Replace vague words and expressions with precise ones that will stimulate the reader's imagination. Invent some concrete details, and replace clichés with phrases that are more vigorous.

The job interview was conducted pretty well. The hiring committee members asked the candidate questions about her past work experience. The candidate explained how her experience could be good for the company. In particular, she explained how she could contribute to improving the firm's profitability by focusing on improving the company's competitive advantage and thinking outside the box. She emphasized win-win strategies based on best practices, which she said would increase the synergy between business units. The members of the hiring committee liked her ideas.

7

Writing
a Persuasive
Essay

Now we come to the final leg of the journey. In this chapter, we talk about how to make your own arguments, sharing your views with an audience. The chapter describes how to write a persuasive essay, but the same process would be used when writing a speech, a letter, an answer to an examination question, or other forms of communication. Writing is perhaps the best way to practise your critical thinking skills — to write, you need to develop your own viewpoint, organize your ideas, collect supporting evidence, and arrange your information logically. You need to be aware of your audience and their beliefs and values, and to build this awareness into the way you present your ideas. By writing, by confronting your ideas outside your own head, you uncover, develop, and clarify your thoughts. You discover what you know. Writing well and convincingly can be the pinnacle of your skills as a critical thinker.

First steps

At the first stage, you need to figure out what your issue is, and what is your position on that issue. This is not a simple as it sounds. Often, a teacher will give you the topic on which you must write, or will give you a list from which to choose. We write best when we care deeply about what we are writing, so your first job may be to discover why you care about an assigned topic. Take the time to think about your own experiences with the issue, especially those experiences that involved an emotional reaction on your part. Emotions, whether positive or negative, signal that an event was important to us in some way, and this can be an excellent reason to choose a topic. Another way to spark your interest in an assigned topic is to discuss it with classmates, friends, or family members. If you discover that a variety of opinions exist, and an animated debate ensues, you have found your topic.

Sometimes you know right away what your claim will be because you have thought about the issue before and have articulated your beliefs. Other times, the claim emerges as you begin collecting your evidence. In the latter case, you propose a tentative claim, and as you collect new information, you keep asking yourself: Why do I think that this claim is true? List your reasons for or against the claim, and eventually you will be able to decide what your position should be. If your claim is a complex one, and your essay is more than a page or so, it is likely that there will be several reasons in support of your claim, and each reason can be treated as a subordinate claim for which you will also need evidence.

Make an outline of your main claim and sub-claims and continue collecting evidence. The amount of evidence that is *sufficient* depends on the complexity of your claim, and how much it challenges the status quo. As a baseline, we will assume here that your aim is to find between three and five pieces of evidence for each sub-claim. As noted in Chapter 3, evidence can come from a wide range of sources, and the wider the range, the better the *representativeness* of your evidence. Books, professional or academic periodicals, websites, business newspapers, interviews with experts, as well as your own experiences as an employee or customer — each of these sources can make a valuable contribution to your argument.

Secondary sources

When you are using books, periodicals, or information from the Internet, try to ensure that the sources you have chosen are reputable. This can be difficult to judge if you do not already know a lot about a topic or field; your instructor or a librarian can help you here. Publications with a long history can generally be trusted more than those marked "volume 1, number 1". Many scholarly periodicals are peer-reviewed, that is, the articles in them are evaluated by experts before they are published. You can therefore have more confidence in these texts than in articles that are not peer-reviewed. Much of the material on Internet sites has not been peer-reviewed, and so is less reputable. Look at the sponsors of a website to determine the potential for bias. Opinions found on commercial Internet sites, for example, may be more subject to bias than those on educational sites. Citing reputable sources increases the *authority* of your evidence. Yet, however reputable the source may be, you want to read their arguments critically before deciding to include them in your own essay.

Critical reading, as you know, requires you to find and assess the quality of the author's argument. Underline the words that locate claims and evidence, as well as words that catch your attention because they are surprising, arouse emotion, or are ambiguous. Examine the quality of the evidence: sufficiency, accuracy, precision, representativeness, authority, and clarity. Annotate the text with your own comments in the margins, making a note when any aspect of the evidence strikes you as particularly good or bad. Also, make a note when you find a piece of evidence that contradicts evidence you have read elsewhere. Make the author's underlying assumptions explicit. If there are reality assumptions or value assumptions that you think you can challenge, make a note of it. As well, be on the lookout for alternative explanations of causal claims. Consider the author's rhetorical style. How has he or she used words to increase the persuasiveness of the piece? In addition, consider the components of the author's argument in light of your own prior beliefs and values. Did you initially agree or disagree with the author's claim? How might this have affected your reading? What do you believe now? **Box 7.1** provides an example of critical reading.

Box 7.1: An example of critical reading

This is an excerpt from an interview with a Montreal entrepreneur. Notice the reader's marginal comments and how his reaction changes from the beginning to the end of the piece. Which comments are related to his analysis of the qualities of the evidence? Which are related to underlying assumptions? What are your own reactions? Are they similar to or different from this reader's?

Claim is in opening (and closing) sentences

Cue words for evidence #1

Family members in the business is a big no-no. The smart entrepreneur will keep his family as far away from the business as possible. Believe me, I've been 36 years in business and I've been burned often. For example I had my ex-wife's sister running my store in the west end. You'd figure this would be someone I could trust, but all I got from her was headaches. Sometimes it was ten o'clock, ten thirty, eleven o'clock, she's not there yet to open the store. I was losing money hand over fist, and in the end, I had to fire her and close the store. As you can imagine, it didn't make me too popular. But what else could I do?

Lots of experience which increases authority. Must be a pretty old guy!

Anecdotal evidence. Vivid narrative style makes it clear and easy to read

Evidence #2

Assumption that lots of time spent with spouse is a negative outcome. What a jerk! No wonder they're divorced.

And that wasn't all. Back in the eighties, my wife was working as my bookkeeper at the downtown store. We'd be together all day long, we'd be eating breakfast, lunch and dinner together, we'd come to work together and go home together. Ninety-five percent of my waking hours were with that woman. It was all too much.

Evidence #3

Implicit assumption that the son is not interested in work.

It's not just wives — all your family take you for granted. Take Victor, a buddy of mine who has a property management business. He worked long, hard hours, nurturing this little business so that finally he made something great out of it. Then he brings his son on board. Big mistake. According to Victor, all the kid wants is to draw a big salary. He sees his father driving a Lexus, he wants one too. He wants to be a chief without ever having been an Indian. What he doesn't understand is that his father has paid his dues. You've got to earn it.

Another anecdote. Is this generalizable?

Phrase evokes sympathy for Victor

Is this racist? I'm not sure, but I don't think I like this guy!

Evidence #4

Evidence #5

Survey is more precise and authoritative than anecdotes

Look at the Eatons. Look at the McCain family. And remember the Steinbergs? Everywhere you look you see family businesses in trouble or going down the tubes. It's not just my opinion. Experts agree that working with family members is a problem. A survey done by a couple of professors in a Montreal business school showed that 54% of the entrepreneurs they interviewed said that working with family members creates problems. Business is business. Right or wrong, you are not your brother's keeper. Family and business don't mix.

I can think of other family businesses that continue to be successful. The Bronfmans, the Saputos, my friend Diana's in-laws.

How many entrepreneurs did they interview? Is 54% high enough for me to buy this evidence? If he'd given the names of the profs, it would be more persuasive.

The phrase makes it sound like he's not really interested in considering any opposing viewpoint. The whole thing is pretty one-sided.

Note: Names and some details have been changed to protect the entrepreneur's anonymity.

After a critical reading of the text, you will take notes of the information you would like to include as evidence in your own essay. Some authors write their notes from each source on a separate index card; this practice allows you to organize the evidence easily and also to change the sequence of ideas if you decide on a different logical order. The cut-and-paste function of your word processing software can also achieve this end. Be sure to include a full citation of the source of your evidence along with your notes. Although direct quotation can be useful, it is best to use your own words to summarize the author's ideas and your reactions to it. Having done your critical reading and annotation, why would you want simply to copy down an author's words? Always paraphrase.

Perhaps not always. Occasionally you may find a brief passage in a text that is vivid and particularly well stated — this you may want to use as a direct quote in your own essay. The rule of thumb is that the quote should be no more than two or three lines of text, and should be so evocative that you want to share the author's actual words with your own readers. Be aware that this should be a rare occurrence. Shakespeare, Cervantes, and the authors of ancient religious texts have created truly evocative writing; material of this calibre is rare in business writing, but if you find it, you can quote it. Be sure to use clear quotation marks and include page numbers for quotes, along with the full citation. All else in your notes should be paraphrased. Remember that you are building your own argument, not just regurgitating large chunks of other people's words. And always, beware plagiarism. See **Box 7.2**.

A fine quotation can enhance the *precision* and *vividness* of your argument. So can relevant statistics, which are easier to find than quotes. Be sure to note the date that the information was collected so that you (and your readers) can judge the currency of the statistics. Detailed descriptions of particular events or activities of organizations also contribute to precision. Finally, do not forget that personal anecdotes can also be relevant evidence. Include these on your note cards as well.

Interviews

You may get the opportunity to interview experts as part of your search for evidence. In business, these may be managers, entrepreneurs, labour leaders, government officials, or other experts. They may also be rank-and-file employees or customers who have experience with particular aspects of the topic you are studying. When collecting evidence via interviews, it is vital to treat interviewees with respect, and to report accurately what you are told. Ethically, you must explain the purpose of the interview and obtain consent before proceeding. You must respect the interviewees' confidentiality, and guarantee that their names will not be used in your report without their explicit consent. In general, you must ensure that there are no negative consequences to your respondents from participating in your interview. Find out about your school's code of ethical conduct for research with human participants and be scrupulous about following the requirements.

Box 7.2: *"Man, what an idiot. What was I thinking?"*

A *New York Times* business reporter, Zachery Kouwe, resigned in February 2010, accused of plagiarizing from the *Wall Street Journal.* When interviewed about his situation, Kouwe confessed that he was shocked to discover that he had plagiarized. He told the interviewer that when he was shown the instances of plagiarism, he said: "Man, what an idiot. What was I thinking?" According to Kouwe, his problem was carelessness. He had copied news stories from the Internet, and he would paste them into computer files as raw material for later use. His mistake was using the same computer files to store material he had written himself. When he was ready to organize and write his own article, he no longer remembered that parts of the stored text had been copied from other sources. In his words, "It was just my carelessness in trying to get it up quickly."

Kouwe is by no means the only journalist who has suffered the humiliation of losing his job for plagiarism. The lesson we can learn from incidents like this is to be scrupulously careful in our note-taking — using quotation marks and writing full citations when we cut-and-paste material — and to avoid the pressure of deadlines by giving ourselves the time necessary to write carefully and well.

Note: For more about journalistic plagiarism, see C. Hoyt, "Journalistic Shoplifting", *New York Times*, March 7, 2010, p. WK10.

In planning the interview, prepare a brief list of questions in advance, ensuring that the wording of your questions allows your interviewee to provide explanations and describe events, rather than just giving "yes" or "no" answers. Sometimes an interviewee will allow you to record the conversation; more often you will have to take notes. If the interviewee says something you would like to quote in your essay, be sure to read it back to him or her so that you can report it accurately. Respect the agreed-upon duration of the interview, and leave contact information so that the interviewee can get in touch with you, if necessary. Interviews can be a rich source of evidence that is *authoritative* as well as *precise*. Include this evidence in your notes, just as you did with evidence from secondary sources. Add the name and a brief description of the interviewee. If the interviewee wishes to remain anonymous, you would describe her in terms of a relevant role, such as "middle-manager in a high-tech company", or "cashier who works the night shift at a 24-hour convenience store".

Organizing your ideas

When you have taken notes for all sources, including your interviews with experts and your personal musings, it is time to read through all your notes and decide on an order of presentation. Group your notes according to your sub-claims, ensuring that the order of presentation is logical. You may want to try several different orders to see which one flows the best. At this stage, you may also notice that some parts of your argument need additional evidence, or you might decide that you need to re-think the phrasing of your claim.

Take the time to ensure that each piece of evidence you have selected is relevant. What underlying assumptions led you to choose these particular pieces of evidence? Are your assumptions so generally accepted that they can remain implicit, or do you need to state them explicitly?

Writing the first draft

Now you are ready to write. Having done all this preparation work, writing is simply the process of getting the words down. For most people, of course, getting the words down is not simple at all! You should not expect to produce perfect prose as soon as you sit down at the computer with your notes. What you will produce is a first draft — rough, inelegant, and probably ungrammatical. This is a necessary first step for the majority of writers, even best-selling authors. Writing instructor Anne Lamott, in her book, *Bird by Bird*, has referred to the first draft as the "down draft", in which you get your ideas down. Later you will work on the "up draft", in which you fix it all up. So don't worry about crafting perfect text at this stage. Resist the temptation to edit your sentences. Just jump in and write the whole thing out.

Put your major claim near the beginning of your text. You will decide later about your introductory statement — it does not have to be the claim — but for now, this will help the focus of your writing. Start a new paragraph with each new idea. Keep going. People use a variety of little tricks to keep themselves writing. For example, some people decide on a length of time (like 30 minutes) or a number of words (like five hundred) and they make themselves continue until they have achieved this goal. A frequent result of even these modest goals is that the words start to flow and you will end up writing considerably more than you set out to do. Some people plan little rewards for meeting their goals, like a cookie or 10 minutes on their exercise machine. Find out what works for you. When you have included all your notes in the paper, write a first draft of a conclusion, usually some form of your major claim.

Finally, collect your citations in a list of references at the end of your paper. A number of referencing styles exist. In the field of business, the APA style is quite common. (An introduction to APA style can be found at <http://apastyle.apa.org/>.) Choose it, or use the style your instructor requires.

Revising

This is the stage at which you polish your text. Reread the entire document to ensure that it is focused and that your argument flows logically. Make sure that your ideas are presented as clearly as possible. Add subheadings and paragraph transitions to help the reader navigate the text.

As you think about your readers, anticipate that at least some of them will have objections that are related to conflicting assumptions and values, or personal experiences that differ from your own. Deal with these potential objections explicitly by rebutting them or limiting your argument. You may also now work on your rhetorical tone, choosing the words that will create the narrative or scholarly impact you would like to make on your audience.

Next, write the opening paragraph. Generally, you want to rouse the readers' interest in the first sentences of your essay, making them keen to continue reading. A vivid anecdote, a description of an unusual event, a startling statistic relevant to your issue — any of these could be a stimulating start to your essay. In you begin this way, be sure to state your major claim explicitly near the end of the introductory paragraph, showing how it is relevant to the anecdote, event, or statistic.

The closing paragraph also has an important role to play. It summarizes your argument, reminds the readers of what they have learned in your paper, and satisfies them that the evidence you have presented supported your claim well. A closing paragraph may also include a summary of recommendations or actions to be taken that stem from your argument.

Finally, check your paper for spelling and grammatical errors. Computer spell-checks do help, but they are not enough. Reading your paper out loud can help you to see missing words and typographical errors that the software might not have picked up. Having a friend read your paper can help with typos, too. Equally important, your friend might find holes in your argument or might find your explanations confusing, and this can lead you to tighten your logic and improve your essay considerably. Double-check your references for accuracy, and for consistency with the style guidelines. Remember that a good list of citations increases the authority of your work.

Images enhance the clarity of your essay

The clarity of your essay can profit from visual aids that enhance your ideas. Recall the discussion of concept maps (Chapter 2) and see if there are diagrams you can create to make a complex claim easier to grasp. You may also want to add tables or charts. If you do, be sure to give them titles and refer to them explicitly in the text. Photographs or clipart can also be added. If you find these on the Internet, they may be copyright-protected, and you will have to get permission to use them. Of course, you can always create your own digital images and include them in the paper. Remember, however, that the visual aids are meant to add to the clarity of your argument. Do not add images just because they are pretty — they have to be *relevant* to important aspects of your claim or evidence. Also, do not use so many images that it distracts the reader from your main ideas.

Lastly, give your essay a clear title that is not too long. Don't try to be so "cute" with the title that the reader cannot predict what the paper is about.

"Writing to change the world"

A final note about persuasive writing — you should never forget that writing is a way that you can have an impact on the world. The problems of business and society are huge and complex, but if you can articulate your ideas for change clearly, and with enthusiasm, you can make a difference. Mary Pipher, the author of *Writing to Change the World*, describes the desire to effect change as an "internal combustion of intellect, heart and experience" (2006: 13). She notes that writing can help you to "clarify your thoughts, experience new hope and new energy ... *[and]* translate your passion and idealism into action" (2006: 42). Good, persuasive writing presents readers with new ideas, new experiences that go beyond their own activities, and alternative points of view. Good, persuasive writing ignites conversation about vital matters and may even propel your readers into action.

It is important to note here that persuasive writing is *not* propaganda. Writers of propaganda want their readers to agree blindly and without thought. Propagandists misrepresent or try to hide alternate viewpoints. When you are writing honestly, on the other hand, you should encourage the reader to see the world more broadly and more accurately. This means that you should include contradictory evidence, questions that have not been resolved, and multiple viewpoints in your writing, but also show the reader how you came to believe in your claim. In Pipher's words, you want to "teach readers how to think, not what to think" (2006: 23).

As a persuasive writer, you want to tell a story that makes your reader care about the issue. This often means writing vividly about the experiences of real people with whom the reader can empathize. It may mean sharing with the reader how and why we developed our interest in the topic to begin with. You need to put a human face on your ideas. Certainly the logic of your argument, the quality of your evidence, and the clarity of your assumptions are vitally important, but if on top of these requirements you can arouse readers' passions, making them feel what you feel, you can be an agent of change. About 20 years ago, the Stanford professor and writer Harold Leavitt famously said that business education can make students end their studies with "lopsided brains, icy hearts and shrunken souls" (cited in Pfeffer & Fong, 2002: 80). Prove Leavitt wrong.

Conclusion

Now your journey really begins. You are ready to explore the huge and growing fund of knowledge available from business magazines, newspapers and books, television documentaries, and motivational speakers, academic journals and Internet blogs. Appendix 1 is designed to help you with this exploration. It presents and explains some expressions that are currently popular in the business literature, with examples of how they are used.

You will soon be ready to contribute to the literature with your own views about business events and activities. As a first step, write a letter to the editor or join an electronic discussion group and present your well-considered opinions on a business issue that interests you. As a fully engaged citizen, or even a future business leader, the world needs to hear from you! Start now.

Appendices

Appendix 1 Business Terms and Popular Expressions

As you read the business news and views, there are terms you will encounter frequently. Here are definitions for a selection of them. For each term, we draw on the current business press to demonstrate how the expression is used, and to give you a sense of why the issue is of contemporary interest.

Board of Directors

A group of people who have the legal responsibility to guide the affairs of a corporation or firm. The principle duties of a board of directors' are the selection and evaluation of the senior management, the establishment of the firm's broad policies and objectives, financing decisions, regular review of the firm's performance, and accountability to shareholders. Sometimes boards of directors are powerful, independent bodies, while other boards may be more submissive to top management, and merely "rubber-stamping" management decisions. Recent unethical behaviour and illegal activities among upper-level executives have drawn attention to boards, provoking much discussion about their duties and responsibilities. A broader term, **corporate governance**, refers to the rights and responsibilities of the board of directors, managers, and owners of a company.

> The **corporate governance** landscape has changed significantly over the past few years ... and altered attitudes within **boards of directors**. There has been a greater effort on the part of board members to get proper training for their roles as active monitoring agents, and the development of a new attitude about how many boards to serve on, and in what capacity.
>
> R. Colman, "Promoting Better Governance",
> *CMA Management*, 80, 1 (March 2006): 44.

> Ideally, **directors** should be intelligent, informed team members and able to stand up to management. In practice the classic criteria still apply, but they are diluted by new, less relevant ones. For example, "good" directors should have training in **corporate governance**, remain alert during long meetings where colleagues probe the smallest details of an activity and be available for less important meetings. This favours the bureaucratic types and eliminates a lot of good candidates.
>
> M. Côté, "Beyond Compliance",
> *CA Magazine*, 139, 3 (April 2006): 64.

Boards naturally believe that the person they have appointed to run their company is more capable than the average boss. Suggesting otherwise by withholding pay rises and bonuses would call their judgment into question. Nell Minow of the Corporate Library, a **corporate-governance** watchdog, may be right that "the only thing that will have an impact on executive pay is giving shareholders the ability to throw out **board members** who get it wrong. Disclosure is not enough."

> Anonymous, "Business: Cheques and Balances; Executive Pay
> in America", *The Economist*, 394, 8673 (March, 2010): 69.

Bottom Line

A summary number that expresses how successful a company has been from a financial point of view. It is a colloquial term for a company's profit, that is, net income. (Net income is the **bottom** or last line of an income statement). More generally, the bottom line can refer to any underlying or ultimate criterion of success. A recent expression, the **triple bottom line**, describes an accounting not only for financial performance, but also for social and environmental performance.

> Catherine Swift, president of the Canadian Federation of Independent Business ... says the government's decision to increase the threshold for which companies qualify for the 12% small business tax rate to $400,000 from $300,000 in income was "the single best thing. That will affect lots of businesses very soon, right on the **bottom line**."
>
> A. Holloway, "Is Everybody Happy?"
> *Canadian Business*, 79, 10 (Summer 2006): 40.

> Many HR practitioners are expected to play a more strategic role to help their organizations adapt to a changing business environment and workforce. Beyond environmental sustainability, switching to electronic solutions can free up HR practitioners' time for bigger-picture, more strategic work. It all translates into less paper usage, better service for employees, more efficient and strategic workflow for HR and even cost savings, which are all contributors to the "**triple bottom line**" — people, planet and profit.
>
> J. MacLellan, "Electronic Solutions a Greener Option",
> *Canadian HR Reporter*, 22, 8 (April 2009): 16.

> Most federally incorporated financial institutions are required to publish a public accountability statement that discloses, among other things, their goals in community development and examples of the activities undertaken on a voluntary basis by employees on behalf of the institution for the purpose of community development. Although this requirement is narrower than full-scope **triple bottom line** reporting, it is a clear step in that direction.
>
> P. Jackson, "Serving Stakeholders",
> *CA Magazine*, 136, 2 (March 2003): 34.

CEO

The Chief Executive Officer (CEO) is appointed by the board of directors to head the firm's activities. He or she sets company policies and a strategic direction to ensure the firm's success. As the highest-ranking manager, the CEO must be familiar with all functions within the organization, and he or she should have strong leadership skills and a clear **vision** (see page 100) for the firm. In some companies, the CEO also chairs the board of directors, and there are mixed opinions of the value of this arrangement. The CEO generally works with a **top management team** of other officers to make the big decisions for the organization. The team may include a chief financial officer (CFO), a chief operating officer (COO), and sometimes a chief information officer (CIO).

When a **CEO** quits his job for "personal reasons," it is usually dismissed as code for an ouster, or at least a sign that simmering differences with a company's board, or perhaps controlling shareholders, have reached a boiling point.

M. McCullough, "The Gen-X CEO Takes His Leave",
Canadian Business, 83, 6 (April 2010): 23.

Equity analysts, whose job it is to scrutinize individual company stocks from every conceivable angle ... have sophisticated, nuanced understandings of the companies they cover, enabling them to ask seemingly arcane questions of **chief financial officers** on conference calls. Yet the worst-kept secret about them is that they rarely advise clients to sell a security, regardless of changing economic or financial conditions, or even a company's individual circumstances, for that matter.

M. McClearn, "Plan for All Seasons",
Canadian Business, 83, 3 (March 2010): 48.

Novell has replaced its top executive amid signs that the latest attempt to revive the software company's flagging fortunes has foundered. Jack Messman, **chief executive officer** and chairman, ceased to be employed by the company on Wednesday, Novell said, though he will remain a director until October. The company also revealed that it had ousted its **chief financial officer**, Joseph Tibbetts. The management upheaval reflects the failure of Mr Messman's strategy to ... return Novell to growth at a time when its traditional networking software business is in decline.

R. Watersin, "Novell Ousts Chief Amid Signs of Strategy Failure",
Financial Times, June 23, 2006, p. 26.

The chair-**CEO** relationship is quite unique: an interdependent relationship of equals at the top.... What makes this relationship work? It certainly helps if the chemistry is right — if the two just "click" and mutual trust and respect is instant. Even if the chemistry is strong — and critically if it is not — the two must recognize that learning how they can best use each other's strengths to the benefit of themselves and the company takes deliberate effort.

R. Hossack, "Together at the Top: The Critical Relationship
between the Chairman and the CEO",
Ivey Business Journal Online, January/February 2006, p. 1.

Emotional Intelligence

The ability to understand and manage your own emotions, accurately perceive and understand the emotions of others, and use emotions competently to sustain good relationships. The term was popularized by Daniel Goleman in the mid-1990s. It is measured as an **EQ** (emotional quotient), which some people believe is more highly correlated with success in every-day life than an IQ (intelligence quotient) score.

> Everyone needs the support and assistance of others. Thus, it's foolish to burn bridges and alienate people you may need one day. Showing an inability to get along with others will virtually eliminate any chance you have of moving up into management one day yourself. The higher you go in any organization, the more **"emotional intelligence"** is expected of you, and this quality reveals itself by your ability to resolve differences between your co-workers in a mature and peaceful manner.
>
> K. Simmons, "Five Ways to Impress the Boss",
> *Office Solutions*, 23, 3 (May/June 2006): 32.

> The first succession plan developed should be for the CEO role. The board is responsible for hiring the CEO and knowing, at all times, who the CEO's potential successors are, whether the candidates are internal or external to the organization. The board should have intimate understanding of the leadership qualities, area of expertise and **emotional intelligence** of each person on the potential successor list.
>
> D. Myers & M. Haeussler, "Succession Planning Going Deep",
> *Credit Union Management*, 29, 3 (March 2006): 24.

> What it takes to get hired is often very different from what it takes to stay employed. Technical skills may win you the job, but poor self-awareness and a lack of **emotional intelligence** can prevent promotion or even result in dismissal. In a study released in 2005, Leadership IQ studied 5,247 hiring managers at 312 companies. The managers made more than 20,000 hires in three years. The findings: Forty-six percent of newly hired employees fail within 18 months. The causes were overwhelmingly employees' lousy interpersonal skills.
>
> L. Wolgemuth, "How to Stand Out from the Crowd and Kick-start Your Own Recovery",
> *US News & World Report*, 147, 5 (May 2010): 14.

Globalization

The steady increase in the extent to which markets, labour, knowledge and technology, as well as commercial, social, and political activities in countries around the world are integrated. Strong links among the world's economies have expanded opportunities for companies to sell their goods and services globally. On the other hand, these links have increased competition world-wide. Playing a role in the trend towards greater globalization is the **multinational corporation**, any organization that operates in two or more countries. The revenues of some very large multinationals, like General Electric, Toyota, or ExxonMobil are comparable to the GDPs of many nations, and this makes them a powerful force affecting business, culture, and politics. There is energetic debate about the advantages or dangers of powerful multinationals and the progress of globalization.

> About 200,000 foreigners went to India for medical and dental treatment last year, a figure growing by 15 percent a year, according to the Confederation of Indian Industry. A report by McKinsey Consulting in New York predicts medical tourism will be India's next boom business, generating $2.28 billion in revenue by 2012. Suneeta Reddy sees it as part of a trend toward **globalization.**
>
> "Establishing Indian medical genius abroad puts India on the world map," says Reddy, executive director of Apollo Hospitals Group, a Chennai-based chain founded in 1983 by her father, Boston-trained surgeon Prathap Reddy. "Not only are we excelling in IT and manufacturing clothes, but up the value chain, we are producing outstanding results in health care. There is a certain amount of pride in that," she says.
>
> P. Yelaja, "India Offers Surgery in a Hurry",
> *Toronto Star*, June 17, 2006, p. A1.

> Many of **globalization's** most vocal supporters have justified the loss of manufacturing jobs in the West on the ground that the rich world will maintain an edge in innovation; the clever jobs will stay at home. Emerging economies are not merely challenging that lead in innovation. They are unleashing a wave of low-cost, disruptive innovations that will, as they spread to the rich world, shake many industries to their foundations.
>
> Anonymous, "Leaders: The New Masters of Management",
> *The Economist*, 395, 8678 (April 2010): 11.

> The economic research division of US investment bank Goldman Sachs ... suggests that the so-called BRIC countries (Brazil, Russia, India and China) ... could rank among the world's top six economies by the middle of the century. "The BRICs are a key aspect of the modern globalized era," say the Goldman Sachs' researchers, adding "what distinguishes these four countries from other emerging markets ... is their strategic importance to **multinational companies** and their centrality in the current wave of **globalization.**"
>
> M. Siddiqi, "Dawn of a New Economic Order?"
> *African Business*, 319 (April 2006): 48.

Knowledge Workers

Employees who work primarily with their intellect and knowledge, and who create value for a firm by processing and creating information. The term was coined by Peter Drucker almost 50 years ago. The supervision of knowledge workers is an interesting management challenge, since the supervisor may frequently have less expertise than his or her subordinates. **Intellectual capital** is a broader term that refers to the set of intangible assets that a company owns or controls. These include, for example, the employees' knowledge and expertise, organizational technologies and processes (documented or undocumented), patents, copyright, and business networks.

As various analysts have observed, the class system is in flux. The blue-collar manufacturing class — semi-skilled, reasonably well-off, protected by strong unions and a paternalistic state — is disappearing, its jobs outsourced to low-wage economies overseas. Many white-collar jobs have disappeared as well, replaced by software and offshore call centres. Instead ... new economic classes have emerged. At the top are **knowledge workers** ... who exploit and profit from an economy that prizes intelligence, creativity and ambition, whether in designing a computer program or an advertising campaign.

J. Ibbitson, "No Easy Solution to the Woes of the Working Poor", *The Globe and Mail*, May 16, 2006, p. A4.

It doesn't make a lot of sense in today's global marketplace to educate the best and brightest and then send them away to England or India or China to start businesses and develop new technologies for US competitors. But that's exactly what current US policy encourages by limiting the employment prospects of foreign students who would rather stay here.... It's unfortunate that the US isn't producing more home-grown talent in [math, engineering, technology or the physical sciences].... The reality today is that the US ranks sixth world-wide in the number of people graduating with bachelor's degrees in engineering. Jobs will leave the US and our economy will suffer if bad policy limits industry's access to **intellectual capital**.

Anonymous, "The Other Immigrants", *Wall Street Journal*, March 27, 2006, p. A16.

People, not products, money or factories, are key to the intangible assets that make up your company's value.... **Intellectual capital** or knowledge capital is not some computerised database. It walks out of the door every evening and you hope it returns in the morning.

P. Hurley, "What Will Drive the Future Workforce?" *Strategic Communication Management*, 10, 1 (2006): 5.

Outsourcing

Delegating some of the organization's activities to an outside manufacturer or service supplier. It is sometimes termed **contracting out** or, when the work is delegated to an organization in another country, **offshoring**. Organizational functions that are outsourced are many and various, including data analysis, human resources, customer service and technical support, accounting, design, manufacturing, and janitorial services. An outsourcing decision is usually taken to cut costs, or when a company prefers to focus on its **core competence**, the central activity and specialized expertise company, that it performs better than competitors and which may bring it long-term success.

Automation and **outsourcing** have claimed whole classes of jobs. Among them are routine but vital tasks that were labour-intensive before the computing revolution: manufacturing and number-crunching jobs that used to pay handsomely. The economy now needs workers to do what can't be done by machines or call-centres in Bangalore, which leaves iPad design and caretaker work but not enough in between.

> Anonymous, "United States: As Jobs Fade Away; The Middle-class Task-force", *The Economist*, 395, 8681 (May 2010): 33.

In its current form **outsourcing** has been employed with great success by companies such as General Electric and Procter & Gamble. While the most common reasons to outsource used to be costs or head-count reduction, today the drivers are more strategic and focus on keeping value-added activities in house where an organization can better utilize its own **core competencies**. Many executives are discovering **offshoring** is about corporate growth, making better use of skilled staff and even job creation, not just cheap wages abroad. Labour savings from global sourcing may still be substantial, but it's minor compared to the enormous gains in efficiency and productivity.

> P. Brent, "The Third-party Solution", *CA Magazine*, 142, 4 (May 2009).

The company provides fruit processing services, protein processing, and in-container processing to name a few. The company's **core competencies** include citrus extraction, coating equipment design, filling and closing, freezing and chilling, labelling, portioning, refrigeration and sterilization. The company also offers breading machines and equipment, fryers, and mixers and slicers for meat and poultry.

> Anonymous, "Worldwide Food Expo 2009: Product and Technology Review", *Food in Canada*, 69, 9 (Nov/Dec 2009): 30.

R&D

Acronym for Research and Development, the activities in a firm that combine scientific research and technological development to produce innovations in products or services. When firms spend a relatively large proportion (e.g., 15% or more) of their revenues on R&D, they are often characterized as "high technology" firms. Many large firms in pharmaceuticals, computer software, biotechnology, etc., have substantial R&D expenditure, although some people believe that small organizations tend to be the most successful innovators.

In my experience, too often there is a giant wall erected between marketing and **R&D**. The development people, the "D" part of **R&D**, almost literally heave a product over the wall to marketing when it is ready to sell. Marketing is the go-to-market lot who then look at what they've been given, scratch their collective heads and wonder who in their right mind will want to buy this gizmo? ... What am I saying? A key challenge for marketing is learning to work more effectively with the innovation machine of your organization. This is extremely true in high-tech but also true in virtually any industry which has **R&D** capabilities. So if you want to wow your customer, go hug an engineer!

K. Moore, "Hug an Engineer Today",
Marketing, 110, 23 (June 27, 2005): 9.

A study in 2005 by consultants at Booz Allen Hamilton, the most comprehensive effort to date to assess the influence of **R&D** on corporate performance, concluded that "there is no relationship between **R&D** spending and the primary measures of economic or corporate success." ... Most of the innovation in pharmaceuticals these days is coming from small new firms. Big Pharma's **R&D** activity is now concentrated as much on identifying and doing deals with small, innovative firms as it is on trying to discover its own blockbuster drugs.

"Survey: The Tortoise and the Hare",
The Economist, 378, 8461 (January 21, 2006): 8.

Our products are animal-free and trans fat free. We're putting about 15 per cent of our sales back into **R&D**.... I think the proportion is very significant for a start-up company like ours. We must continuously improve and refine our products and that's the only way you can survive in the marketplace.

S. Eagle, "Food in Canada + KPMG: Executive Roundtable",
Food in Canada, 64, 7 (September 2004): 33.

Shareholders

Part-owners of the corporation. These are people who have invested in a company, and have been issued shares in the company in proportion to their investment. Although every shareholder is an owner, large companies may be owned by millions of shareholders, so most individual investors would have very little say in the policies of such a company. The job of the **board of directors** (see page 92) is to look after the interests of the shareholders. **Stakeholders** are a broader group of people who have an interest in the firm because they are influenced by its actions. This group includes shareholders, but also the firm's employees, customers, and suppliers, and even the government and the community in which the firm is located. A company that is sensitive to the needs of its stakeholders is said to have good **corporate social responsibility**, although some believe that attention to stakeholders may erode the rights of shareholders.

"It's hot to be green," said Tom Arnold, Chief Environmental Engineer for TerraPass, a company that invests in clean, renewable sources of energy. As concerns grow over global warming, environmental pollution, dwindling stocks of fossil fuels, and the role of corporations within society, more attention is being paid to **corporate social responsibility**.... More and more consumers and **shareholders** are putting pressure on corporate board members and executives to care about how their companies impact the environment and society.

T. Diana, "Doing Business the Socially Responsible Way",
Business Credit, 108, 6 (June 2006): 45.

Almost all companies that have tried to elevate the interests of particular **stakeholders** above those of the long-term **shareholder** without protection have had financial problems.... The Body Shop's focus on environmental and social objectives at the expense of more conventional goals almost brought the company to its knees. **Shareholders** whose interests are sacrificed to those of other **stakeholders** will almost certainly move their money to more attractive opportunities elsewhere.

A. Likierman, "Stakeholder Dreams and Shareholder Realities",
Financial Times, June 16, 2006.

It's hard to avoid Lee Scott's tender side these days. In April the Wal-Mart chief executive told a convention of journalists that he plans to build stores in high-crime neighborhoods, in run-down malls, even on contaminated land. Why? Not because these are the best places to put a store. The idea, said Scott, is to "engage the community," reaching out to poor folks and minorities, the kind of "people and neighborhoods that need Wal-Mart most." ... Then there's Anne M. Mulcahy, boosting morale by telling Xerox employees to take their birthdays off. Or General Electric's Jeffrey R. Immelt, refusing his last cash bonus in favor of performance-linked shares to show that he's aligned with shareholders.... And a new breed of execs, including Alan G. Lafley of Procter & Gamble, has started to talk more about the concerns of "**stakeholders**" who feel the impact of a business, instead of just **shareholders**.

D. Brady, "Charm Offensive",
Business Week, 3990 (June 26, 2006): 76.

Embracing **corporate social responsibility** is not only good for a company's image, it's also good for its **bottom line**. That's because adopting **corporate social responsibility** can raise the organization's profile in the community and boost employee loyalty and engagement.

A. Mercy & A. Dailey,
"Recognizing Good Deeds Provides Its Own Rewards",
Canadian HR Reporter, 19, 7 (April 10, 2006): 8.

Vision
An image of the future held by leaders of the organization. Some organizations have vision statements that describe, in vivid terms, the goals they wish to achieve. A related term is the **mission statement**, which is a broad statement of the purpose of the business, the firm's reason for being, and the underlying values that animate the organization. Although many agree about the importance of having a vision, some believe that vision and mission statements are frequently empty "motherhood" statements that have little impact on a firm's actual goals or activities.

Nearly two-thirds of Canadian employers surveyed by Catalyst, a New York-based research and advisory organization that promotes women in business, have a stated commitment to diversity in their **mission** or **vision statements**. However, that commitment hasn't translated into practical application, said Deborah Gillis, Toronto-based vice-president for Catalyst in North America.

S. Klie, "Firms Short on Diversity Practices: Report",
Canadian HR Reporter, 22, 6 (March 2009): 3.

The Calgary Exhibition & Stampede is embarking on an ambitious $500-million, multi-year master plan to transform itself into a world-class destination. Now all it needs is a master brand and marketing strategy to provide the road map as it moves beyond its famous 10-day summer rodeo and fair to becoming, according to its **mission statement**, "a gathering place for Calgary, Alberta and the world, 365 days a year."

M. Ramage, "Steering the Stampede to a New Frontier",
Marketing 111, 18 (May 15, 2006): 11.

It was one of those rare moments of candour you get when dealing with senior management. "I know that our **mission statement** talks about innovation and creativity," an executive once hesitantly told me. "But we really don't want people thinking outside the box. We just want to make the box cheaper." Translation? She wasn't really interested in innovation and creativity. She just wanted to keep costs down.

M. Rosenberg, "Moving Beyond the Mission Statement",
Canadian HR Reporter 19, 7 (April 10, 2006): 18.

Leaders who bring the best out in their followers ... are inspirational. They communicate a compelling **vision** that others enthusiastically embrace to fulfill a common higher moral purpose. [The middle manager's] ... role is to personalize the organization to the employee. You are the one who brings personal meaning to the **vision** and organizational goals espoused by senior executives.

R. Hackett, "Bring Out the Best",
Canadian Business 79, 12 (June 5–18, 2006): 73.

Appendix 2 Comprehensive Exercises

EXERCISE 1: REAL ESTATE STAGING ————————————

Read the text critically and answer the questions that follow.

Real estate staging is the business of improving the look of a home so that it is more appealing to potential home buyers. Stagers suggest ways that sellers can invest a small amount of money to have maximal impact on the physical appearance and "ambience" of their homes. Paint jobs and minor repairs, removal of clutter, window cleaning, and strategic use of colour and placement of artwork are a few of the recommendations stagers make to increase the market value of a home. Stagers often get their clients on the recommendation of real estate brokers.

The price of staging ranges widely, depending on the extent of involvement of the stager. A simple consultation in which the stager goes from room to room making recommendations, can cost the home seller between $350 and $500. A full-blown staging project can include painting, moving furniture, bringing in borrowed furniture, hanging curtains and pictures, and even shopping for necessary supplies, such as bedspreads and new towels. This generally requires that the stager hire one or more assistants. The pricing model is based on hourly rates — the lead stager may earn $75–150 an hour and the assistants, $25 per hour.

Ms. Nairn Friemann has a successful staging business, but she feels that a major drawback is her difficulty in charging clients a fair price. Here is what she said in an interview:

> It was a real eye opener this year to find that my prices are way below the competition. I find out what others charge because we sometimes bid on some jobs and afterwards the brokers tell me what others had bid. For some jobs I charge $2,500, so it is not like I charge nothing. It's just that I hear after that others charged $6,000 for the same level of service. And I thought that $2,500 was good!
>
> I charge more than the minimum, but where I have done myself out of a lot of money is when I hear the sad stories, or it is an elderly couple, or it is a widow. Whenever I hear sad stories, I always try to make it okay for the home sellers — I try to keep the price down. But if I charge $2,500 for a project fee, and other stagers charge $5,000 or $6,000, that is a big difference. And when I am charging someone a few hundred dollars to shop, I feel I should not be charging them a mark-up on the items as well. But a lot of stagers do. They will charge a 10% mark up on the stuff they've bought.
>
> Sometimes it is the brokers who persuade me to have low prices. The broker may have a client who is not willing to pay for the staging but she

really wants the house to look good for the photos. Well, she may give me a lot of work. Do I make an exception? In one case, it turned out to be 16 hours of shopping, bringing plants, doing the prep, dealing with the photographer, and moving stuff all around the terrace so we could get some good shots. Sixteen hours and I got $600. That kind of job, I should walk away, but it is a broker who gives me a lot of work, and that is another issue. I want to keep the brokers happy because they send me clients.

In any business based on hours, you can become a commodity. Instead, you have to charge on the value of what you are delivering. I did an online coaching session about how to charge more, get what you are worth, and how to build your business. One of the things the coach said is that she never gives anybody a price right away when they ask. And she gives people three levels like silver, gold and platinum or whatever. So I have changed my pricing to three levels. My basic price is the staging plan. It is a good option. The better option is collaborative — the property owner does some of the work and I do some. And then I have the total freedom package, where in most cases I should be able to charge $10,000. I do the total staging, I manage their move to the new place, I make sure that their furniture gets delivered and set up in a really nice way. That is what the money is for; there is real value in that. So that is how I am trying to reorient the way I charge.

The online coach also said that before she gives a price, she asks the person what their goals are. If you and I were to work together, she says, what would it be worth to you if we were to accomplish these goals? And that makes them think of the value of selling and that puts them into a whole different thought process, away from the question of how many hours it would take. I walked away from one consulting job because the woman asked how much do I charge per hour, and then proceeded to tell me that the job should not take more than two hours. That way you are not being compensated for your ideas or expertise. So I am trying to get away from the concept of the hourly rate.

My problem with pricing must be a personality flaw. Sometimes I think that among entrepreneurs in general, women have a harder time charging than men. Somebody suggested that I should function like the advertising agencies: I will be in charge of creative and I should get someone to be in charge of billing. Even when I do invoicing, I am reluctant to throw in another $500; I am always short-changing myself so that I can make it work for other people. Some of the staging that I have done had huge value; it is crazy what I am charging.

Interview with Nairn Friemann of "Ingenuity and Pizzazz",
conducted by Christopher Ross and Linda Dyer,
February 2010, Montreal.

QUESTIONS

1. Identify Ms Friemann's main claim, and evaluate the evidence, underlying assumptions, and persuasiveness of her argument.

2. What is your reaction to the idea that there is a gender difference in setting prices? If you had to collect evidence to support or refute this claim, where would you look? What sources of evidence would build the best possible case for your viewpoint?

EXERCISE 2: LET'S DROP THE PENNY ─────────────

Read the text critically and answer the questions that follow.

The Canadian dollar was created about 150 years ago, and divided up into 100 cents. At that time, legislators thought about further dividing it into 1,000 mills, but they decided it was not useful: the cent (now commonly called the penny) was a small enough unit. In those days, a labourer working for a day might earn a dollar, so it was necessary to divide the dollar up into smaller units, and the penny was reasonable as the smallest unit. Today, however, someone working at minimum wage for a day will earn about 50 dollars. One one-hundredth of a minimum day's wage is now 50 cents and for most people it will be more. Why do we need a penny? It is approximately one-five thousandth of the minimum daily wage. One hundred and fifty years ago, our politicians didn't see the use of a coin one one-thousandth of the typical daily wage. Why do we need one even smaller?

People routinely throw away pennies, or put them in jars and forget about them. In fact, a 2007 survey found that only 37% of Canadians actually use pennies. Yet, because of the law, the Canadian Mint must go on making hundreds of millions of pennies every year. Worse, experts have estimated that it can cost well over a penny to make a penny coin; the annual cost is $130 million or more. Pennies are an enormous waste of money. They are also a huge waste of time. Have you ever stood in line behind some very old or very young person carefully counting pennies out of a purse? If you have had this experience even once, you can appreciate why there is a legal limit to how much you can pay with pennies. For example, don't try to pay for a week's groceries using only pennies — the cashier would refuse to accept them and he or she has the right to do so.

Why don't we eliminate the penny? Because some people are afraid that if we get rid of the penny, merchants will take advantage of the situation and round prices up but not down. But this does not make sense. Gasoline is priced in 1/10th of a cent — mills in fact — but you don't need mills to buy gasoline, and nobody is worried about that. Your final price is rounded down or up according to a standard rule. Things are priced in pennies because pennies exist. Also, sales taxes at will always create final prices in fractions of whatever the smallest unit of currency we have, but some will be rounded down, some up, and in the end it will average out.

There are very real costs to continuing to use the penny. It's expensive for the Mint to make the coins; it's expensive for banks and merchants to count them. Moreover, for the shrinking percentage of people who actually use them, they are heavy, breaking pockets and purses. And they are time consuming for everybody.

QUESTIONS

1. Identify the main claim and evaluate the evidence, underlying assumptions, and persuasiveness of the argument.

2. Interview 15–20 people about their reactions to getting rid of the Canadian penny. Develop your own claim and write a persuasive essay on this topic.

EXERCISE 3: THE TOCO PORT AND FERRY SERVICE ——————
Read the text critically and answer the questions that follow.

The author thanks the curators of the Toco Folk Museum for providing the information on which this report is based.

The Government of Trinidad and Tobago, a two-island republic in the southern Caribbean, recently announced plans to establish a new ferry service. The ferry will run between Tobago, the smaller island which is 30 miles north-east of Trinidad, and Toco, a small coastal village on the north-eastern tip of Trinidad. The current stage of the project is that a developer has been selected, and all that remains is to negotiate the terms of a final agreement. This proposed development, if it goes ahead, will replace the current ferry service between Tobago and the capital city of Port of Spain, which is on the island of Trinidad. It will also radically change economic, social, and environmental life in the Toco region. As such, it must be very carefully considered, with the involvement of the widest possible range of stakeholders in the debate.

The village of Toco lies in a pristine natural setting. Rainforests stretch into the hills to the west and south. Many residents cultivate small agricultural plots in the forests, providing subsistence and a basic income. The ocean beyond, the meeting point of the Caribbean Sea and the Atlantic Ocean, is the site of Trinidad's only coral reef. Fishing is a major source of livelihood in the community, though declining fish stocks and the threat posed by large commercial fishing interests are an ever-present problem for the small fishermen. In recent years, eco-tourism has been a growing alternative to farming and fishing, the traditional methods of generating income. Nesting grounds for the giant marine leatherback turtles, the nearby beaches have great potential as an eco-tourist destination.

How does the proposed port and ferry service fit in this picture? Evidence from usage statistics of the existing ferry from Port of Spain indicates that the ferry is used primarily by Tobagonians who are travelling to and from Trinidad to transact business — they are market vendors, building contractors, hardware dealers, and other business people shopping for consumer goods and building materials. Relocating this service in Toco will require a dredged harbour, a jetty, parking for a large number of cars, trucks and containers, turn-around facilities, warehouses and hotels. Almost all the ferry traffic, passengers and freight, will be going to and from Port of Spain. Toco is currently a two-hour drive from Port of Spain, mainly along a narrow, winding coastal road. Miles of wider roadway will have to be built to accommodate trailer trucks and much heavier traffic. All of these developments will utterly change the face of Toco and the surrounding region.

The plan envisages reclaiming from the sea two to three hectares of land on which these facilities will be built. What will be the impact of this land reclamation on the fragile reef system? How will the diverted sea water be handled in order to avoid coastal erosion, flooding or the salination of rivers? What are the plans to manage industrial effluent and other pollutants? There is no evidence that environmental impact studies are being carried out. In any case, there are many examples which prove that government watchdog agencies lack the "teeth" to curb the excesses of commercial interests. How is this apparently lackadaisical attitude consistent with Toco's emerging eco-tourism activities?

Other outcomes must also be considered. Many farmers in Toco cultivate ancestral lands for which no property deeds exist. With the proposed developments, land values are sure to rise. What will be the protection for these deed-less farmers from unscrupulous land speculators? We can learn a lesson from Tobago here — with the large-scale development of tourism in the past two decades, many residents of the island of Tobago have found themselves marginalized, no longer able to afford the escalated property values that came with the influx of European and North American currency.

Should the ferry project go ahead, a rise in population is to be expected, and there will be a severe strain placed on existing health and social services, public utilities, schools, policing, transport and other community facilities. Currently, many of these services are close to primitive; substantial improvement will be necessary if the proposal goes through. Yet, in a meeting with a Toco community leader, the Minister of Works declared that private commercial interests will be funding the project entirely, and "the government will not be spending a cent". This statement, meant as an assurance, is cause for alarm. Moreover, the government negotiating team that is responsible for the final agreement with the developer, has no representatives from the Toco community.

No doubt the building of the facility will provide employment for young people, most probably as labourers. While this may seem advantageous, it is definitely a short-term benefit. Once the facility is complete, labour needs will be for skilled workers, and few of the Toco workers will be able to compete for these jobs. Chances are, however, that they will be reluctant to return to fishing and farming. And even if they are interested in returning to their old lifestyles, they may find that their land has been expropriated and that fishing is less viable than it was. The government has stated that longer-range plans for the region include the building of a heliport, bunkering facilities for gas and oil, a marina for pleasure craft, and a cruise ship terminal. Clearly, little thought has been given to the needs of the community. Preferred development would be in ecologically aware, small-scale industries that draw on local skills and the available natural resources to create long-term employment and economic development. Such industries might include the manufacture of paper, rope, woven mats and brooms from the native grasses, pottery products made from available clays and sand, and a variety of organic products such as fertilizers and animal feed (from seaweed), and spices, herbal preparations and cosmetics (from the varied plant life that is abundant in the area). Heliports and cruise ships are not harmonious with Toco village life.

In a community newsletter, Edward Hernandez, the curator of a Tobago museum, noted that the social impact of rapid development in Tobago has included a rise in theft and crimes against persons, drug trafficking and drug use, and an increase in prostitution, sexually transmitted diseases, and mental health problems. In conclusion, it is vital that we learn from the lessons of recent history and reconsider this ferry project. Development, yes. But development that empowers the local community, preserves the natural environment, and allows the people of Toco a viable future.

QUESTIONS

1. Identify the main claim and evaluate the evidence, underlying assumptions, and persuasiveness of the argument.

2. Do some research within the broad topic: "Economic development in emerging nations". Search for articles reflecting a broad representation of views, which may include articles written by academics, journalists, and environmentalists — stakeholders in developing as well as developed countries. Based on your reading, develop a specific claim about a particular aspect of economic development. Write a persuasive argument related to your claim.

Appendix 3 Answers to Selected Exercises

Exercise 2.1

1. *Claim: Working in your field before entering university leads to academic, career, and life success.* Your statement of the claim may not use these exact words, but the sentence should involve both pre-university work experience and various types of success. The indicator words, "it is my view that", in the third sentence and, "as a result", in the sixth sentence signal that key parts of the claim will follow. This is a contestable claim.

3. *Claim: Too much choice makes it unlikely that people will act.* The indicator words, "it may be helpful to realize", signal a conclusion. You may have used the word "crippling" (from the second to last sentence) in your claim. This is not necessarily wrong, but since the word is metaphoric, it is better to use plain language that can be understood independently of the text. This is a contestable claim, despite the use of the words "in fact" in the last sentence.

5. *Claim: Testing consumer products on animals must stop.* This is the first sentence of the paragraph that explicitly presents the author's thesis. It is a contestable claim. You may have strong beliefs that the claim is correct. If so, remember that a claim believed to be true can still be described as contestable. In other words, justification must be provided; a simple statement of the claim is insufficient. Without evidence, claims like this run in to the dead-end of "My opinion against yours".

Exercise 2.2

The unproblematic claims are #3, #6, and #8. All the others are contestable and will need to be justified. Remember that you may be in full agreement with a claim, but it is still contestable.

Note: #7 is interesting because it is usually seen as an unproblematic, common sense statement. This unproblematic claim is made contestable, however, by Alfie Kohn in his 1993 *Harvard Business Review* article entitled "Punished by Rewards". Kohn argues that rewards do not differ much from punishment in that they are manipulative and create a workplace where people feel controlled. They make employees compete with one another and encourage them to conceal their shortcomings from their supervisors. Rewards discourage risk-taking, learning, and progress. Finally, psychological research shows that rewards actually undermine intrinsic interest in the job. Recipients come to see rewards almost like bribes; they perceive themselves as working because of the salient reward, rather than because of their own enthusiasm for the task.

In the same vein, Richard Farson (*Management of the Absurd*, 1996) believes that "praising people does not motivate them". Again, he argues that all evaluation makes us uncomfortable, even positive evaluation. The person giving the praise is, by implication, standing in judgment over us. Moreover, praise is frequently used as a "sugar-coating" for reprimand. Parents and teachers are always using the "sandwich" technique which recommends that you say something nice before and after giving criticism. The result is that we have become conditioned to brace ourselves for reprimand whenever we hear praise.

Both these authors, then, provide us with reasons to label #7 as a contestable claim.

Exercise 3.1

Claim: Bottled water has no safety benefits and can contribute to pollution, so sales are dropping.

Evidence: NRDC report on undeclared use of tap water in bottles; rates of contamination; expert opinion on plastic bottles and recycling rates.

Accuracy: Do you have information about bottled water contents that is independent of what you read here? Do you and the people you know regularly recycle water bottles? Perhaps you have read about this issue or seen documentaries about it on television. If so, you will have an independent basis for judging the accuracy of the information here.

Precision: The figures about consumption of bottled water, the amount of water needed to produce bottles, and the recycling rate do help to increase our confidence in the accuracy of the evidence. In particular, the statement about the 72 billion gallons of water that are required to produce the plastic bottles gives the impression that research was done to come up with that number. On the other hand, we are given no idea of the significance of this number with respect to the total volume of water bottled. In addition, precision would have been improved with fewer "round" numbers like "more than 100 brands" or "less than 20%" recycling of bottles. The "per capita consumption of about 20 gallons" should have specified whether this was annual consumption.

Sufficiency: The evidence for environmental problems and contamination may be sufficient for a text of this length, but there is insufficient evidence about dropping sales. No figures about changes in sales over time are provided, so this part of the claim is not convincing.

Representativeness: The text refers to North American as well as worldwide evidence. On the other hand, most of the evidence comes from institutes that embrace the environmentalist cause — one begins to wonder whether the inclusion of a neutral source of information might have been desirable. Testing over 100 brands seems to be a good-sized sample.

Authority: The Globe and Mail is a well-respected newspaper, and citing the work of researchers like Dr. Todd Jarvis, who clearly have expertise in the field, is persuasive.

Clarity of expression: The claim was clearly stated, and the evidence was presented in readable prose.

All in all, on the basis of your own assessment of concerns like those listed above, you would decide how persuaded you are by the text.

Exercise 3.3

Claim: Employee satisfaction is bad for productivity.

Evidence: Report of a research study with 149 employees and the researcher's comments on her findings.

Accuracy: You should think about whether you have any independent knowledge of people who are creative on the job, people who voice their complaints, or those who do well or poorly in competitive environments. If you have been an employee yourself, think about times when you have been happy or dissatisfied, then think about whether these explanations make sense to you.

Precision: There is little or no use of numbers in this text. Precision might have been strengthened by presenting some of the statistical evidence on which this conclusion is based. Perhaps, too, a quote from a particularly satisfied or dissatisfied employee could have been used to emphasize the impact on productivity, creativity, or problem solving.

Sufficiency: The evidence is all drawn from a single research survey of 149 employees. This is fairly typical of popular newspaper reports of scientific research, but it is still just one study.

Representativeness: There was no additional information about the 149 employees, such as what types of jobs they had, and what industries they worked in.

Authority: The use of Professor Zhou's title throughout the piece, the phrase "rigorous research", and the specification of the university at which she works increase the authority of the work. If you have heard of Rice University and believe it to be a good school, that would increase authority further.

Clarity of expression: The claim was clearly stated at the start of the text. By the end of the text, however, the recommendations are vague and somewhat puzzling, and this detracts from clarity.

All in all, on the basis of your own assessment of concerns like those listed above, you would decide the extent to which you are persuaded by the text.

Exercise 3.5

1. Get Bank of Canada statistics on electronic fund transfers. Search for newspaper reports on the volume of e-commerce transactions. Interview firms about the volume of Internet sales compared to in-person sales, and how this has changed over the past 10 years. Survey a sample of consumers about their buying habits and how they have changed over time.

3. Review the social work literature to find academic articles about the issue. Conduct interviews with elderly people and their children or neighbours. Interview doctors or psychologists who can provide expert views. Talk to veterinarians and pet trainers who might have useful input.

5. Ask a sample of young adults about their living arrangements, and the reasons why they live where they do. Interview a sample of parents of grown children about the choices made by their offspring, as well as the choices the parents themselves had made when they were the same age as their children. Search for relevant information about "heads of households" in Statistics Canada data, and check for changes over time. Talk to real estate agents about their experiences with customers, and get their impressions of changes over time. Look for news reports about the issue.

Exercise 4.1

3. Wives should ensure that their husbands are well-dressed. Alternatively, spouses are responsible for each other's presentation.

5. Entrepreneurs owe it to their children to offer them jobs in the business. Alternatively, relatives should have priority for jobs in family businesses.

7. Chinese people know good Chinese food.

Exercise 4.2

1. **Claim:** Commercial advertising should be allowed in universities.
    Evidence: Senior administrators want funds from corporations; ads are everywhere; students and staff say they are not affected.

    Assumptions:

    (a) *Senior administrators should be the ones to make the decisions about accepting commercial advertisements.* This may be a value assumption held by people who respect those in authority, or who think that senior administrators are best placed to see the "big picture" of university functioning. For these people, the evidence would be relevant. The evidence might be seen as irrelevant by people who believe that senior administrators do not spend a lot of time in classrooms or common areas, and so they might underestimate the impact of the ads. Such people might prefer the views of students or teachers who spend considerable time in the areas where the ads are located.

    (b) *The university is just one more place, like everywhere else, so it is okay that it has ads like everywhere else. The evidence is relevant.* The alternate viewpoint is that the university, as a centre of education, is special. You would not expect to see commercial advertising in a church, temple, or court room — the ideals of religious and legislative institutions are different. Similarly, the ideals of educational institutions make them special places. The presence of advertising on the streets and public transport vehicles is irrelevant.

    (c) *The presence of ads has no effect on people. If they are not distracting, they should be allowed.* On the other hand, it could be argued that people are often unaware of the effects of ads, so we cannot rely on their say-so that the ads are not problematic. For example, should we therefore feel free to expose our students to subliminal persuasion to get credit cards or expensive cars? Without knowing it, they (and we) could be wooed into debt.

3. **Claim:** Accidents in office workplaces are increasing.
    Evidence: Description of types of accidents reported in past five years; more people are texting while walking.

    Assumptions:

    (a) The writer is assuming that the *increase in accidents is not simply a matter of a larger number of people working in office settings or a greater tendency to report accidents.* To evaluate this reality assumption, we might ask about the accident rate relative to the number of office workers, as opposed to the simple frequency of accidents. Has the rate increased proportionately?

(b) It might also be argued that over the years people have been increasingly likely to expect personal safety and attention and compensation for minor injuries, and so they may be more likely to report these types of accidents.

(c) It is *because of the increased frequency of texting while walking that accidents are on the rise*. This assumes that because both accidents and texting have increased over the period, that the second is the cause of the first. As we will see in Chapter 5, it is not necessarily the case that an increase in two phenomena means that one has caused the other. For example, there has also been increased concern about physical health over the period, and perhaps people are more likely to take the stairs from floor to floor, or at least to run for the elevator, which might lead to an increased accident rate. Similarly, if the workplace has become more crowded because companies are trying to save money on office space, people might be more likely to collide. We cannot be certain that texting is the major factor explaining the rise in accidents.

(d) A complete ban suggests that *people only text while walking*, but this is unlikely. Moreover, some people might take issue with this recommendation because it treats employees like infants, not adults. Instead of a ban, companies should simply alert employees to the dangers of texting while moving about, and rely on their good judgment to act appropriately. This last objection is value-based.

5. **Claim:** Smokers who go against the advice of their doctors should be placed last on hospital waiting lists.
   Evidence: British doctors do this; the Canadian health system is over-extended.

   Assumptions:

   (a) *Doctors are authority figures who should be obeyed.* People who value respect for authority would be likely to agree with this assumption. People who think individual freedom is more important would be less convinced.

   (b) *Sick smokers who continue to smoke should be punished.* Yet some people see smokers as victims themselves — tobacco companies are the real culprits because they have "hooked" people at a young age, and now these people find it extremely difficult to quit smoking.

   (c) *The behaviour of British doctors and the British National Health Service are appropriate role models for Canadians.* It may be countered that Canada should be setting its own priorities in managing health care, not just following the lead of another country.

(d) *If the system is over-extended, we should react by making lists of priorities.* It can be argued, however, that more money and other resources should be put into the system, rather than just agreeing to make do with less.

Exercise 5.1 (Part I)

In general, the more diverse, plausible explanations you thought of, the better. Here is a sample of causal explanations that other students came up with.

1. You've overslept three times in the past week.

   Sample causal explanations:
   - I've been up late every night, studying or partying with friends and I'm tired.
   - My alarm clock must need a new battery.
   - I may be coming down with a cold or something.
   - The seasons are changing and my body is reacting to changes in temperature, light, or humidity.
   - There's something I have to do that I'm unconsciously avoiding.
   - This is an improvement — I usually oversleep every day.

3. It takes you an hour to finish an exam that is scheduled to last for three hours.

   Sample causal explanations:
   - I studied hard and know my material well, so I sailed through the exam.
   - The exam set was not long enough for the scheduled time.
   - I went too fast and carelessly because I was worried about time from the start.
   - I didn't know the answers to most of the questions.
   - The exam paper I got was missing the last three pages.

5. Although overall industry sales are down, your product is exceeding projected sales figures.

   Sample causal explanations:
   - My product is superior to the competition.
   - My sales force is exceptionally good.
   - I underestimated my budget figures.
   - Marketing and advertising strategies have paid off.
   - My product is in a specific niche where the target market is growing relative to the population (e.g., seniors).
   - My clientele is more faithful than average.

7. You didn't get the promotion you feel you deserved.

Sample causal explanations:

- I've made mistakes I'm not aware of, but my boss knows about them.
- Company policy says no-one gets promoted before a year in a position and I've only been here six months.
- Bad timing — I asked at a time when sales figures were down.
- The company is being restructured and they are trying to flatten the hierarchy.
- Unfair preference was given to someone less deserving.
- My expectations were unrealistic (e.g., I think everyone is stupid except me and I should be president).

9. One of your less-talented subordinates is invited to lunch by your boss.

Sample causal explanations:

- The subordinate is going to be fired and they're doing it gently.
- The boss being a mentor, helping the subordinate to improve.
- The boss is attracted to the subordinate and is trying to develop a personal relationship.
- They are already friends, unbeknownst to me, and they're just lunching together to enjoy each other's company.
- The person is more talented than I realize and is going to be promoted.

Exercise 5.2

1. **Claim:** The uncertain economy is causing the incidence of workplace aggression to rise. The **causal explanation** offered: When people feel deprived of expected amenities or when they are fearful of losing their jobs, they become stressed and this causes them to be violent and abusive.

   Rival causal explanation: Perhaps the author is correct, but perhaps this is an example of the *post-hoc fallacy* at work. Just because the increases in workplace aggression followed the economic meltdown of the mid-2000s, this does not mean they were necessarily caused by the economic problems.

   It is possible that the passage of workplace psychological harassment laws, beginning in the middle of the decade, have made it more likely that people would report aggression at work. Similarly, an increase in media reports of aggressive incidents or a general increase in the self-esteem of employees might lead to greater reporting of these incidents. Moreover, some researchers believe that people are spending longer periods of time at work, and their increased fatigue might be contributing to increased aggression.

Some of these factors may have started having their effects at about the same time that the economic condition worsened. Any one or some combination of them might be causing aggression, independently of the economic meltdown.

3. **Claim**: Having family-friendly policies makes firms more profitable. The **causal explanation** offered: Employees are happier and more focused on their work, so they are more productive.

   Rival causal explanation: The author has explained the *difference between two types* of firms — those that have family-friendly policies and those that don't — by focusing on one possible difference between the two groups of employees. This explanation is quite plausible, but there may be other differences between the two types of firms that we should consider.

   For example, firms with family-friendly policies also tend to be large, established firms with human resource departments. Profitability, then, is explained by the size of the firm — large firms enjoy economies of scale, for example, and are generally more profitable than smaller firms. In this case, the feelings of the employees and their family concerns may be irrelevant. In other words, if size and family-friendly policies tend to go together, it is hard to tease apart which of these two factors may be causing profitability. It may even be both.

   It is also possible that profitable firms can afford to be more generous with their employees, offering them perks that are not possible for firms where budgets are tight. This explanation is akin to *reverse causality*; profitability precedes (and causes) family-friendly policies.

5. **Claim**: Requiring board members to own large blocks of shares increases profitability and share prices. The **causal explanation** offered: Board members who own shares then have a financial interest in the company. They can be expected to do their best to ensure that the firm does well.

   Rival causal explanation: There is a correlation between the two variables and the author is assuming that one (share-ownership) is causing the other (share prices). The most plausible rival explanation is based on *reverse causation*, perhaps share prices are causing share-ownership. More specifically, it may be the case that when a company is doing well, the directors decide to buy shares.

   It may also be argued that when board members hold a significant number of shares, employees are aware of this and it increases their confidence in the organization. They are therefore motivated to work and their hard work will improve profitability. In this case, *the direction of causality is the same* as the author proposes, but *the underlying explanation is different*.

117

improves their chances. We must ask: Are there any other likely differences between these two groups?

One such difference is that employees would be most likely to refer people whom they think would be competent. Suggesting the name of someone who turns out to be a poor performer reflects badly on the referee. Chances are, then, that the group of people who were referred had higher skills than the group who were not referred. After all, anybody can send a resume in to a bank, however good or bad their qualifications. Thus, it may be the better qualifications of the referred group that led to an elevated hiring rate, and nothing at all to do with insider information.

Exercise 6.1

This exercise is something of a classic; variants of it are frequently used in class demonstrations. Did you find that the different people you talked to gave you very varied answers? What might be some of the reasons for this variety? Often it is because people of different ages and backgrounds have very different experiences which lead them to view the world through totally different lenses.

The exercise shows the importance of providing precise, concrete details in your writing. When you use vague words, the images people get in their heads can be quite unpredictable!

Here are some answers provided by a few people known to the author. Hannah and Lori are high-school students, aged 15 and 17 respectively; Barry is 20 and is an undergraduate student studying for his B.A. degree, while Maura is in her mid-20s and attends graduate school in business. Susan is a 47-year-old teacher and Mr. P is a 60-year-old accountant.

name	middle-aged	high-paying	large city	low-paying	small town
Hannah	40	$400,000	300,000	$45,000	100,000
Lori	35	$250,000	3 million	$75,000	3,000
Barry	38	$100,000	1 million	$30,000	30,000
Maura	55	$150,000	400,000	$50,000	6,000
Susan	45	$90,000	25 million	$15,000	1,000
Mr. P	40	$50,000	500,000	$25,000	100,000

References

Boorstin, D. (1961). *The Image*. New York: Harper & Row Publishers.

Booth, W., G. Colomb, and J. Williams (2008). *The Craft of Research*, 3rd edition. Chicago: University of Chicago Press. [The listing of the various aspects of the quality of evidence draws on the work of the authors.]

Chaffee, J. (2000). *The Thinker's Way*. Boston: Back Bay Books.

Lamott, A. (1994). *Bird by Bird: Some Instructions on Writing and Life*. New York: Anchor Books.

Micklethwait, J., and A. Wooldridge (1996). *The Witchdoctors: Making Sense of the Management Gurus*. New York: Random House.

Pfeffer, J. & C. Fong (2002). "The End of Business Schools? Less Success Than Meets the Eye", *Academy of Management Learning and Education,* 1, 1: 78–95.

Pierce, J., and J. Newstrom (1996). "Interview with L. Cummings". *The Managers' Bookshelf*, 4th edition. New York: Harper Collins.

Pipher, M. (2006). *Writing to Change the World*. New York: Riverhead Books.

Rushkoff, D. (2009). *Life Inc.: How the World Became a Corporation and How to Take It Back*. New York: Random House. [This book traces the history of the corporation, from its birth 400 years ago, to its current status as a dominant influence on modern life.]